# *Learning to Live*

*Learning to Live*

By the same author
*Learning to Pray*

# Learning to Live

## EVAN PILKINGTON

Darton, Longman and Todd
London

First published in 1987 by
Darton, Longman and Todd Ltd
89 Lillie Road, London SW6 1UD

© 1987 Evan Pilkington

ISBN 0 232 51757 6

British Library Cataloguing in Publication Data

Pilkington, Evan
    Learning to live
    1. Christian life
    I. Title
    248.4      BV4501.2

    ISBN 0–232–51757–6

Phototypeset by Input Typesetting Ltd, London SW19 8DR
Printed and bound in Great Britain by Anchor Brendon Ltd,
Tiptree, Essex

# To Puck

# Contents

# Acknowledgements

Thanks are due to James MacGibbon for permission to quote 'Not Waving but Drowning' from *The Collected Poems of Stevie Smith* (Penguin Modern Classics) and to Mark Pilkington for the photograph of the author on the back cover.

# Part One

## . . . with the Negatives

# 1

## *Fear*

Most of us have hangups of one sort or another. They are a drag, impeding our freedom and growth. We need to understand them, to learn to live with them, to make allowance for them and, as far as possible, to get on top of them: to prevent them from dominating and diminishing our lives.

Most of our hangups come under the heading of 'irrational fears'. There are many such fears. They take different forms and affect different areas of our life. Here is a list of some of them, together with a brief description. See if any of them ring a bell with you.

*The fear of blame*
This shows itself in a hypersensitiveness to blame and criticism and disapproval on the one hand and to praise and approval on the other. When we are blamed, we go to pieces. We wither and die. But when we are praised, we flourish like the flowers in spring.

Fear of blame may lead to anxiety about whether we said or did the right thing. We are for ever wondering what other people are thinking and saying about us.

We tend to justify ourselves all the time, to make

excuses. We can even be driven to tell lies in an attempt to escape being blamed.

Under the influence of this fear we can produce illness which will gain from other people, if not approval, then at least sympathy.

### The fear of guilt

This shows itself in an obsession with sin, involving us in endless introspection and self-examination. This may take up most of our prayer time.

It can drive us into perfectionism, into trying to achieve ultra-high standards, followed by a sense of guilty failure.

It leads to puritanism. We feel guilty if we are enjoying life, if we are happy and comfortable.

We may sometimes wonder whether we have committed the sin against the Holy Spirit, 'the unforgivable sin'. We are not quite sure what it is exactly, but we are anxious in case we have committed it!

### The fear of incapacity

We dread being unable to cope, that we shall fail, that we are not up to scratch. Fear of failure dominates our mind.

We dread new things, new situations. We feel that we shall have to prove ourselves and panic in case we are found lacking. We become very tense and anxious.

We have no confidence in ourselves and our abilities.

This fear is often accompanied by envy and jealousy of those who *can* cope – the beautiful, the successful, the good.

*The fear of insecurity*
This shows itself in a diffused anxiety. We are not quite sure what it is we are anxious about – we are simply anxious! Something is going to go wrong just around the corner.

We dread change of any kind.

We are afraid of death.

As an insurance policy against this fear, we may be tempted to pile up and to cling on to possessions. In extreme cases, we might be tempted to steal.

*The fear of sex*
This fear poisons all natural sexual feelings with a sense of guilt.

We are frightened of sex, shocked by sex, puritanical about sex.

We may feel full of moral indignation about sexual offenders.

*The fear of being unloved*
We feel unwanted, of no value, unaccepted and unacceptable.

In reaction to this fear we become withdrawn, introverted, depressed. Sometimes we may feel suicidal.

On the other hand we can become aggressive, on our high-horse, attention-mongering.

We are oversensitive to and hurt by the slightest rebuff and apparent rejection.

If we should ever be given love – as by a miracle, it seems to us – we cling on to it and become very possessive and jealous.

As a compensation for this fear we can become promiscuous.

In despair about ourselves and our own value, we can be cruel and brutal and hurt other people – getting our own back, so to speak.

I have called these fears irrational because they are based not on reason but emotion – buried emotion. These irrational fears have their roots, their origin, in our unconscious memory. They are hangovers from childhood hurts and fears.

We were hurt, made to feel afraid, when we were young: by being blamed, perhaps violently; or made to feel guilty, perhaps unjustly; to feel inferior and incapable, perhaps in comparison with an older or younger brother or sister; to feel insecure, perhaps because of a broken home or the death of a parent; to feel afraid of sex; to feel unloved, unwanted, unaccepted and unacceptable.

We buried the hurt and the fear: that is what a child does, because it is too painful to carry. But we did not forget it. It became a wound, a sore spot in our unconscious memory, making us unduly sensitive and vulnerable to that kind of thing. So when someone or something touches that sensitive spot, it opens and bleeds, and we cease to be us – a grown man or woman – and become the hurt and frightened little child we once were.

How do we come to terms with these irrational fears?

First of all, understand yourself. Understand your background, understand how the pattern works. If you can trace back your particular fear to a particular incident or situation in your childhood, so much the better. Understand that it is natural, almost inevitable, that you, with your particular background and experience, should react as you do to blame or guilt or failure or insecurity or sex or to a sense of being unloved and unlovable.

You should not be cross with yourself about this. Be as gentle, understanding and sympathetic with yourself as you would be with another person in the same situation.

Secondly, refuse to be bullied by this fear. Refuse to have your life dominated by what is in fact a hang-over from childhood, the memory of a long-buried hurt and fear.

You cannot prevent it from coming into your mind, nudging your elbow, whispering in your ear. But you need not settle for it. Set your will against it. Refuse to entertain it, to dwell on it. There is a Buddhist saying: 'You cannot avoid birds flying round your head, but you need not let them build a nest in your hair.'

When you are aware of this negative fear-reaction, move on quickly to a second reaction. Change the subject. Think of something else, something positive. But you cannot do this while lying in bed with your eyes closed, or sitting in a chair looking into space. Switch on the light and read something. Get up and do something. Switch on the radio, put on a record, look at the telly – anything which will engage your mind and distract you.

Thirdly, it is very important – as a protection against irrational fears – to keep rested, to try not to become overtired and overstrained.

Overtiredness and overstrain open the door of our

unconscious memory and through that open door the old fears pour through, clouding our mind like thick fog. Overtiredness and overstrain debilitate the will, so that we have no power to shut them out, to switch them off. They take control of us and we are powerless against them. When we become overtired and over-strained, we cannot see straight. We get our sums wrong. Two and two make seven. A smile becomes a sneer.

Fourthly – and most important of all – try to substitute faith for fear. Build up your faith in God, brick by brick: faith in his love and in his power.

I shall be writing more about faith later. But I should like to make two points here.

If we are the victims, the prisoners of irrational fears, there will be a negative, cold tap dripping in our mind all day long: I'm not . . . I can't . . . It won't . . . We need, therefore, deliberately to turn on the warm tap of faith to counteract it: God is . . . God can . . . God will . . . We need to have some faith-phrases on the tip of our tongue and to say them to ourselves regularly throughout the day. Such phrases as:

I am of value to God.
I am understood by God, accepted by God, loved by God, here and now, just as I am.
I can do all things through Christ who strengthens me.
Underneath are the everlasting arms.

It is also important that we should put our faith into action; that we should make little experiments and adventures of faith.

For example, when we are plagued with some

anxiety, hand it over to God – 'Father, into thy hands' – and leave it there. But back it will come into our mind and back it must go to God, over and over again. We must keep on repeating the exercise and not be discouraged.

Another example is when we have to go somewhere or do something and we are plagued with the fear of our own value and our inability to cope. Make a leap of faith. Jump in and have a go. Shivering and quivering, I walk into this room, I go up to this man or this woman. Shivering and quivering, I answer the telephone, I write a letter, I set myself to do what I have to do, believing deep down that God is with me and that God will uphold me and see me through, that God will use me with this person and in this situation. And when the action is completed, offer it to God and try to leave it there. Get on with the next thing.

There is an unexpected bonus for people whose lives are haunted by irrational fears.

Once we have come to understand the fears and learnt to live with them, patiently trying to substitute faith for fear, then God can use us. He can use us as his instruments to help other people. People will see that we understand, that we are sympathetic. Instinctively, they will know that they can talk to us. And they need someone to talk to. It is part of their healing.

Thus, as so often in this life, good comes out of evil. Crucifixion is followed by resurrection.

# 2

## *Self-hate*

People who suffer from self-hate have a minus quantity in their bloodstream. They are tormented with a sense of worthlessness. They feel unloved and unlovely, unaccepted and unacceptable. They display all the symptoms I have described under 'The fear of being unloved'. They are also affected by blame, incapacity and guilt. All these fears, turned inwards, produce self-doubt, self-contempt, self-loathing, self-hate.

Such people are very sensitive to the slightest criticism or disapproval, because each occasion reinforces their built-in sense of being of no value.

They find it very difficult to handle love. They cannot imagine how anyone could love them, ever. And if somebody should, then they become overdependent upon that person, overdemanding, possessive and jealous. They need constant reassurance, an overplus of acceptance, approval and praise to make up for the minus quantity which they carry around inside themselves. This leads, obviously, to great difficulties in friendship and particularly in marriage. Too much is expected of the other person. He or she is treated as a god or a goddess, whereas in fact they are just ordinary human beings with limitations and needs of their own.

In their religion, such people tend to be introspective, scrupulous and guilt-ridden.

They can also become perfectionists. Despairing about themselves as they are, they try to achieve some ultra-high standard, in the hope that they will be accepted: justification by works. They attempt to earn, to deserve value, acceptance and love. But it is a vain attempt. They fail and are back at despair-point.

Such people react to self-hate in different ways, according to their temperament. They may withdraw into themselves and be on the defensive. Or they may become aggressive, projecting their frustration, resentment and despair onto other people, onto society, onto the system. Or they may put on an act and aim to please. Perhaps Stevie Smith's poem, 'Not Waving but Drowning', best describes this:

> Nobody heard him, the dead man,
> But still he lay moaning:
> I was much further out than you thought
> And not waving but drowning.
>
> Poor chap, he always loved larking
> And now he's dead.
> It must have been too cold for him, his heart gave
>   way
> They said.
>
> Oh no no no, it was too cold always
> (Still the dead one lay moaning):
> I was much too far out all my life
> And not waving but drowning.

Such people may compensate for their lack of personal

value by greed of various kinds: overeating, over-drinking, overspending.

They often fall into moods of depression, which is a form of submerged rage against themselves. Sometimes they punish themselves masochistically. And they are tempted to murder themselves by suicide.

Sarah, in Graham Greene's novel, *The End of the Affair*, is obviously riddled with self-doubt verging upon self-hate. She writes in her journal:

> If one could believe in God, would he fill the desert? I have always wanted to be liked and admired. I feel a terrible insecurity if a man turns on me, if I lose a friend. I don't even want to lose a husband. I want everything, all the time, everywhere. I'm afraid of the desert. God loves you, they say in the churches, God is everything. People who believe that don't need admiration, they don't need to sleep with a man, they feel safe. But I can't invent a belief.

No, but you can respond to a belief. You can respond to the belief that *God* loves you, the whole of you; not just your 'good' side, but your 'shadow' side, here and now, just as you are. *That* is the Christian belief, the Gospel, the Good News about God which Jesus brought into the world.

There is a paradox about Jesus. He seems to demand perfection of his followers: 'You, therefore, must be perfect, as your heavenly father is perfect.' And yet, he accepted into friendship with himself people who were a hundred miles off perfection: a dishonest tax-collector, a prostitute, moral and social outcasts, a close and trusted friend who betrayed him, a convicted thief. That is one of the things his enemies had against him, that he was 'the friend of tax-collectors and sinners'.

Christians equate friendship with him as friendship with God, acceptance by him as acceptance by God. For, as St Paul wrote, 'God was in Christ reconciling the world to himself'. As St John's Gospel puts it: 'He who has seen me has seen the Father.'

We can sum up the love of God revealed in the life and death and resurrection of Christ, in three sentences. God is Love. The love of God is unbreakable. The love of God is unconquerable.

Apply that to yourself, make it personal.

God loves you, here and now, just as you are.

Nothing you can do can break God's love for you. On Calvary, Jesus prayed for those who crucified him: 'Father, forgive them, for they know not what they do.' Even in that situation of rejection, hatred and cruelty, the love of Jesus still held. And Jesus is the revelation in a human life of what God is like.

The love of God conquers both sin and death, overcomes that which separates. 'Nothing', St Paul wrote, 'can separate us from the love of God in Christ Jesus our Lord.' His love will ultimately conquer all. It will be victorious. It will win through, even in you.

This belief, surely, should be good news to people suffering from self-doubt, self-contempt, self-loathing, self-hate. This Gospel, surely, should bring rescue, release, liberation for people shut up in that prison – however long it takes and however many setbacks occur along the way to freedom.

There was a door
And I could not open it, I could not touch the
    handle.
Why could I not walk out of my prison?
What is hell? Hell is oneself.
Hell is alone, the other figures in it
Merely projections. There is nothing to escape from
And nothing to escape to. One is always alone.
T. S. Eliot, The Cocktail Party

But we need not stay in hell. We need not be alone. We need not stay shut up in that prison of self-loathing and self-hate. We can walk through the door. We can escape. For if God accepts me, just as I am, I ought to be able to accept myself. If God can bear to live with me, I ought to learn to live with myself, the whole of myself, the light and the dark side, a little more peacefully, understandingly, acceptingly.

A friend of mine, Geoffrey Paul, who died not long after having been made Bishop of Bradford, said once in a sermon at a cathedral school service in Bristol: 'I was a shy, timid boy, converted at the age of thirteen. The first effect of that was to enable me to accept myself a bit more, not to have to imitate other people, because I was accepted by God.' To accept the love of God by faith, to accept oneself as accepted by God: that is conversion and its first-fruits. As St Isaac the Syrian wrote, in the seventh century: 'Be on peaceful terms with your own soul and then heaven and earth will be at peace with you.'

I need not fear that in thus accepting myself and learning to live with myself peacefully, I shall grow complacent and self-satisfied. That is the last thing which happens to people who suffer from self-loathing and self-hate.

Take transformation of character. Just as you usually get nowhere with another person merely by being cross with him or her, so you get nowhere with yourself merely by being cross with yourself. You win people, usually, by gentleness, patience, understanding and sympathy. In the same way, people who suffer from self-hate have to learn to be gentle, patient, understanding and sympathetic with themselves, if ever their character is to be transformed. H. A. Williams wrote in his *True Resurrection*: 'Jesus told us to love our enemies, for by loving them we may turn them into our friends. This applies supremely to the enemy within. For our worst enemy is always ourselves.'

In the second of the two great commandments in the New Testament, we are told 'You shall love your neighbour as yourself'. We tend to put all the emphasis on 'You shall love your neighbour' and to slide over the words 'as yourself'. Why? Perhaps because we are afraid of loving ourselves. Perhaps we think that self-love means self-centredness, the root cause of all sin. But there is a true and a false self-love. False self-love is narcissistic, being in love with your own image. True self-love is simply accepting yourself as a person of value. Moreover, until you can accept yourself as a person of value, you will be incapable of loving your neighbour. You will be either on the defensive or the aggressive, protecting yourself or asserting yourself against him or her. You will not be free to love your neighbour objectively. As Eric Fromm, a post-Freudian psychologist, wrote in *The Art of Loving*:

If it is a virtue to love my neighbour as a human being, it must be a virtue – and not a vice – to love myself, since I am a human being too . . . The idea expressed in the biblical 'Love thy neighbour as thyself' implies that respect for one's own integrity and uniqueness, love for and understanding of one's own self, cannot be separated from respect and love and understanding for another individual.

I remember, when I was a young man, going to hear Fr John Groser, famous London East End priest, preach in the University Church in Oxford. He glared at us, pounded the pulpit and thundered: 'I am of value because God loves me and it doesn't matter twopence what *you* think about me; that is the truth about me.'

I *can* love myself, I *should* love myself, because *God* loves me, here and now, just as I am. That is the ground and the source of my value. And if only I can trust his love for me, then bit by bit I can free myself from the self-hate which imprisons, blinds, poisons and destroys. Free to be myself, to let myself go. Free to see and to hear the world around me, without being for ever on the defensive or the aggressive or putting on an act and aiming to please. Free to be open and receptive to God and to God's other children. In other words, free to love God and to love my neighbour as myself.

Canon Gonville ffrench-Beytagh, formerly Dean of Johannesburg, put all this very well in a passage in his book *Encountering Light*:

What distinguishes a Christian from anyone else is not that he goes to church, or that he is good, or that he has been baptized, but that he knows that he, John Smith, is loved and valued at a depth beyond any human imagining and that he desires to respond to that love. He may feel almost filled with hate and lust and envy but he knows he is loved – the whole of him, not just the 'good' bits – and so he can begin to open himself to God and his fellow-men and allow the power of divine love to flood through him.

The priest who wrote those words has not always lived in the sunlight. He has also encountered darkness. Imprisoned at one time in South Africa, he has been a victim of depression. Some years ago he wrote a pamphlet, entitled *Facing Depression*, which has helped many people. The fact that he could write so positively about the love of God, having experienced both darkness and light, should be an encouragement to those of us who are struggling to escape from the dark prison of self-hate.

# 3

# *Anxiety*

Anxiety is a destructive thing. It destroys our concentration. It wastes our time and drains our energy. We are unable to concentrate fully on what we are doing, because half the time we are worrying about the past or the future. We waste our time and tire ourselves out with fantasy daydreaming.

We worry about the past: about whether we said or did the right thing; about how so-and-so is reacting, what he or she is thinking about us. We worry about the present: whether we can cope with what we have to do; what to say and what not to say. We worry about the future: how are we going to manage? what is going to happen? and suppose this happens, then what? There is no end to these seductive murmurings. 'This is what wears the brain tissue and disorders the whole nervous system', wrote Fr George Tyrrell in a letter to Baron von Hügel, 'not study, nor thought – but worry.'

Anxiety attaches itself to all our irrational fears: to the fear of blame and criticism; to the fear of guilt; to the fear of inferiority, incapacity and failure; to the fear of not being loved and accepted; to fear of the future and of things going wrong.

Anxiety is not always self-centred. We worry about other people. A mother worries about her son, a father about his daughter. And vice versa. We worry about the state of the world. We read the newspapers, listen to the radio, watch the TV news, not just with interest and concern but with anxiety and dread. Our anxiety about other people is full of imaginings and we always imagine the worst. We do not live in the real world. We live in a dark fantasy world of what *might* be. So we are unable to be objective, and we fail to be in a position to help the people we are worrying about. Our mind is already clouded by our anxious foreboding.

Money is no insurance against anxiety, as the anxious lives of the rich so often show. 'For', as Kierkegaard wrote, 'riches and abundance come hypocritically clad in sheep's clothing, pretending to be security against anxieties, and they become then the object of anxiety.'

Education is no insurance against anxiety. For anxiety is a nervous and emotional reaction, not a rational response to experience.

Even human love, that most healing and secure-making of human things, is no insurance against anxiety. For human love is, by definition, human; and therefore fallible, imperfect and mortal. It has feet of clay.

Perhaps behind our anxiety there is the sneaking feeling that 'It all depends on me'. But it does not. It depends on God. 'Cast all your anxieties on him, for he cares about you' (1 Peter 5:7). His is the only safe, secure basket into which we can put our 'eggs', those fragile insecure 'eggs' which so trouble and disturb our anxious minds.

In what we call the Sermon on the Mount, Jesus pointed to the natural creation as evidence of the upholding, sustaining love and power of God. If the birds of the air and the flowers of the field, the humbler parts of creation, get by, upheld and sustained by the love and power of God, will not *you*, the peak of creation, also get by, upheld and sustained by the same creative love and power?

Nature is untidy, apparently disorderly, and yet underneath there is order, pattern and growth. In his monumental study of evolution, *The Phenomenon of Man*, Teilhard de Chardin stressed the unity of creation underlying all the apparent complexity and multiplicity. Dylan Thomas said the same thing in a poem:

> The force that through the green fuse drives
>   the flower
> Drives my green age.
> The force that drives the water through the rocks
> Drives my red blood.

'If God so clothes the grass of the field which today is and tomorrow is thrown into the oven, will he not much more clothe [uphold, sustain, drive] you, O men of little faith . . . Therefore I tell you, do not be anxious about your life.' And your life includes your concern about other people and about the world in which you live and of which you are a tiny part.

Instead of losing your powers of concentration, wasting your time and draining your energy by nail-biting, fantasy-building anxiety, put your trust in God.

Find your security in his love and power. This is the only way to escape from anxiety's tentacles, by switching your mind off the anxiety when it comes and switching it on to God; and to go on doing that 104 times a day.

This is not magic. It is faith. And very often it is faith in the dark. Sometimes it seems to be nonsense. But remember, Jesus did not say 'Trust God and you will be all right, Jack and Jill. Say your prayers, practise your faith and you will be successful in business, successful in love, and live to a ripe old age. You won't get cancer, you won't have a nervous breakdown, your husband, your wife won't leave you, your children won't die, they won't take drugs, they won't get into trouble.' Jesus was not such a fool! After all, he warned his closest followers: 'In the world you have tribulation.' And he himself was rejected, betrayed, deserted by his friends, falsely accused, unjustly condemned, tortured, crucified, apparently forsaken by God. Yet it was at that moment that the resurrection happened. 'In the world you have tribulation; but be of good cheer, I have overcome the world.'

You may fail in business, your marriage may break up, you may get cancer, you may have a nervous breakdown; your children may be killed in an accident, they may take drugs, they may get into trouble. These things will hurt you dreadfully, but they will not be the ultimate things, the end of the road. They will not destroy you; just as rejection and suffering did not destroy Jesus. Crucifixion will be followed by resurrection.

Moreover, you will know that you are not alone in your suffering, utterly bereft and forsaken. 'The eternal God is your refuge and underneath are the everlasting arms' – underneath everything, ready to catch you and uphold you. 'Yea, though I go through the valley' – of failure, desertion, disappointment, sickness, tragedy, bereavement – 'I will fear no evil, for thou art with me.' The German poet, Rilke, wrote a poem called 'Autumn'. It is not difficult to imagine leaves falling from trees:

> We are all falling – this hand's falling too,
> All have this falling sickness none withstands.
> And yet there's always One whose gentle hands
> This universal falling can't fall through.

To believe that is faith. To live like that is the escape route from anxiety.

But what about all the evil and suffering in the world, so much of it innocent suffering? So often in this century it has been the men of peace who have been murdered, while the men of ruthless power have flourished like a green bay tree. What about wars and rumours of war? What about natural disasters, failed crops, famine and poverty? Is there not reason for anxiety in such a world as this? We are told that we should put our trust in God, but what is God up to? Is he asleep? Or perhaps there is no God? We are tempted to think that sometimes, when we read the news of the world; that there is no order in the world, no sense and no purpose in life, no God. We are not alone in thinking this. Faith, by its very nature, always has to live with doubt and it will be invaded by doubt from time to time.

I read a novel by a Japanese Roman Catholic,

Shusaku Endo, called *Silence*. It is about persecution in Japan in (I think) the seventeenth century. The chief character is a Jesuit priest on the run. He had gone out to Japan full of faith, but he gradually became obsessed with what seemed to him to be the silence of God in the face of all the innocent suffering. If God *is*, why is he so silent? Why? Why? Why? Tormented by this question, he comes to experience the fellow-suffering of God-in-Christ. I shall quote a few sentences:

> 'My God, my God, why hast thou forsaken me?' It is three o'clock on that Friday; and from the cross this voice rings out to a sky covered with darkness. The priest had always thought that these words were that man's prayer, not that they issued from terror at the silence of God . . . Now in the darkness, that face seemed close beside him. At first it was silent, but pierced him with a glance that was filled with sorrow. And then it seemed to speak to him: 'When you suffer, I suffer with you. To the end I am close to you.' 'Lord, I resented your silence.' 'I was not silent. I suffered with you.'

The suffering of God. I first came across this idea in a book by Studdert-Kennedy when I was seventeen or eighteen. And it changed me from being a God-hater into becoming a Christian. The suffering of God was an unfashionable idea then. Indeed, it was regarded as heretical. But now it is theologically acceptable. Jürgen Moltmann has written a book called *The Crucified God*. Kenneth Leech has a chapter with the same title in his book, *True God*. You will find the same idea in David Jenkins's *Living with Questions*. Moltmann writes: '. . . the theology of the suffering God is more important than the theology of the God who is "wholly other" ' ('The Trinity and the Kingdom of God').

Faith in God is not faith in an Absolute, Unmoved and Unmovable Being, remote from and uninvolved in all the evil and suffering in the world. Our faith in God is faith in God revealed in Christ. God-in-Christ came into this world, lived in it, taught and healed in it. He was rejected by it, suffered in it, was crucified by it – 'crucified amidst universal jubilation', as Kierkegaard put it. But that was not all. God-in-Christ triumphed over the worst that evil could do. He was raised from the dead, Christus Victor. He ascended into heaven where now he reigns. Yet still he bears the marks of his suffering. It is in *this* revelation of God that we are to put our trust: in God crucified, and therefore able to suffer with us in our sufferings and in the suffering of the world. In God raised up from sin, suffering and death, and therefore able to rise up again in us and in the life of the world. In him is our peace and our security.

Peace and security are what we most need if we are victims of anxiety. They are what anxiety robs us of. Jesus said: 'Do not be anxious about your life.' But you *will* be anxious unless you 'cast all your anxieties on him' in the faith that 'he cares about you'. And you *can* trust him, Christ crucified and risen. He is beside you and suffering with you and conquering in you. So, let go your anxieties in faith, drop them like red-hot coals and try instead to concentrate upon what you are doing. In other words, try to live in the present, in the here and the now and not in the past or the future. Jean-Pierre de Caussade was one of the most influential spiritual writers in eighteenth-century France. His advice to people afflicted with anxiety was to leave the past to the mercy of God and the future to his providence, and to try to concentrate wholly upon what he called 'the sacrament of the present moment'.

*4*

*Tension*

Tension can be a great driving force. But it can also overdrive us, making us rush and tear, burning up our energy and wearing us out. Hence its danger.

Tension is the opposite of tranquillity, a virtue much recommended by spiritual writers. Here are two random quotations: 'Everything that has to do with God or the things of God should be done sweetly, tranquilly and without effort' (Jean-Pierre de Caussade). 'Remember that the Holy Spirit works always in tranquillity and even the most devout fuss is not any good to him at all' (Evelyn Underhill). But unfortunately, many of us are anything but tranquil, except possibly in our times of prayer – and not always then. We are often very tense, some of us more than others. In fact, nervous tension is a real problem for some people.

We tend to blame exterior factors – the particular work we do, difficult colleagues or neighbours, the pressures of bringing up a young family, the environment in which we live. And we think: if only I had a less pressured job, I should be able to relax. Or, if only this colleague or neighbour who gets on my nerves and drives me up the wall were to leave, I should be all right. Or, when the children go to school, life will be easier. Or, if only I lived in the country away from all the ugliness and noise of the city, then I should be more peaceful. Or, when I retire and the pressures are lifted, then I shall be free from tension and able to live a quiet, tranquil life.

But is this true to experience? Yes and no. Obviously the removal of exterior pressures does help a lot. But it is not the whole answer. A friend of mine was Warden of a theological college. Each day he would check his letters, sign them and then rush to catch the post in a state of great tension in order to be back in chapel in time for evensong. When the theological college closed down and the pressure of meeting deadlines was lifted, he found that he was doing precisely the same thing with his personal correspondence! I had the same experience myself. When I came to retire and the exterior pressures were lifted, I found that I was transferring my nervous tension onto something else – for example, writing a chapter of this book! This shows that tension is not only due to exterior pressures; it is also interior, something inside ourselves.

Where does it come from? Partly, I think, from our temperament. Some people are temperamentally placid, while others are temperamentally tense. Again, there are perhaps two different types of personality, what I call the extensive type and the intensive type. The extensive type is a quantitative sort of person, able to spread himself or herself over a very wide area without its taking too much out of them. They can get through a vast quantity of work and have many things on the go at the same time. The intensive type, on the other hand, is a qualitative sort of person, a person who uses up a vast amount of nervous energy over every single thing he or she does. And just because they put so much nervous energy into it, there is a certain vivacity, zest and sparkle about whatever they do. But they cannot cope with quantity. They are limited as to the number of things they can take on and they are unable to have too many things on the go at the same time. I am not suggesting for a minute that one type of personality is better, more valuable, than the other. They are simply different, with different strengths and different limitations. But tension is more likely to be a problem for the intensive, qualitative type of person than for the extensive, quantitative type. Again, if we are the victims of irrational fears, for example the fear of blame, the fear of incapacity, we shall be more liable to tension. Fear will drive us to pull out every stop in order to succeed at all costs and against all odds.

How, then, do we deal with tension? Strangely enough, we do not always know that we are being tense. But our husband, our wife, or our close friends know! They see all the physical signs – the clenched fist, the hunched shoulders, the veins standing out on our forehead. And they tell us to relax, to stop getting all tensed-up, to calm down, to turn the kettle off before it boils over. We must try not to resent this. They are not 'getting at' us. They are simply anxious about us, knowing what tension does to us. We should be grateful for their concern, accept their warning, stop whatever we are doing and slow down.

We need to accept and respect the sort of people we

are. If by temperament you are a tense rather than a placid person and if you are what I have called an intensive, qualitative type rather than an extensive, quantitative type, then you have to learn to limit yourself, to accept your limitations. You have to learn to say 'No'. Otherwise, you will have too much on your plate and you will not be able to cope. You will become progressively overstrained, and overstrain is dangerous: it is what leads to nervous breakdown.

Dr Reginald Somerset-Ward was my spiritual director for many years. He once said to me, 'For you, the word No is more pleasing to God than the word Yes.' I must confess that I did not always take his advice. But when I did not, I always paid for it afterwards. How stubborn and foolish can you get! Because of his long experience of dealing with people who became overstrained and then broke down in their middle years at the height of their powers, he was very strict about one's having what he called a rule of rest, which he regarded as important as having a rule of prayer. A rule of rest meant a minimum of seven and a half hours in bed every night and a complete day off each week. To break this rule was a sin, 'the wasting of God's substance'. A rule of rest is a protection. We simply cannot afford to burn the candle at both ends – which is what we are sometimes tempted to do if we are tense, intensive personalities, anxious 'to get through'. If we do, we shall become overtired and overtiredness debilitates the will. The trapdoor on to our unconscious memory will fly open and through that open door will pour all our buried fears and phantoms. Our debilitated will is unable to do anything about it and the fears will take us over. We shall become fear-ridden as well as overstrained.

Tension builds up throughout the day. By lunchtime, we shall have used up quite a lot of nervous energy. It is a good thing, therefore, to have a break at that time. A break will put a wedge in, enabling our battery to be recharged. This after-lunch break really does pay dividends.

It is also important to *stop* when you find that you are getting all tense and strung-up. You cannot do anything properly in that state, so stop whatever you are doing and do something else. Make yourself a cup of coffee, sit down and read the paper, go for a walk round the garden – or the office, or wherever you are – put on a record, listen to the radio: anything rather than push on through the tension.

Some years ago, I went to a conference with the rather pompous-sounding title of 'Society, Stress and Salvation'. The speakers were all very boring, except one: R. F. Hobson, Consultant Psychiatrist at Manchester Royal Infirmary. Bob Hobson is a fellow-Lancastrian who has kept his Lancashire accent. He began by reading a Lancashire dialect poem, and it sounded like a foreign language to all the southerners in the audience. He then proceeded to explain the meaning of three key-words – 'throng', 'thrutched' and 'powfagged'. He said, 'When I go down to the hospital on a Monday morning, I say to my secretary, "Ee, Jean, I feel throng". By that I mean that I'm afraid my coping mechanisms are beginning to fail. But then I say to myself, "Come on, Hobson, you're a Lancashire lad. You just pull a stop out and get on with it". The following Monday, I go down to the hospital and

I say to my secretary, "Ee, Jean, I feel thrutched". By that I mean that my coping mechanisms are actually failing. I can't concentrate. I can't think straight. And worse than that – I'm beginning to get my patients all muddled up. But I say to myself, "Now come on, Hobson, pull yourself together". The following Monday, I go down to the hospital and Jean takes one look at me and she says, "Bob, you're powfagged". And that's when they wheel me into my own psychiatric unit'! His advice was, for goodness sake STOP on 'throng'. Stop whatever you are doing. Be humble. Give yourself a break. Because if you don't, you will move on to 'thrutched'. And if you still go on, you will finish up 'powfagged'.

A friend of mine sent me a critical blurb about a car which he had come across in a motoring magazine. The car was described as 'noisy when pushed'. He added the comment, 'This strikes me as a neat description of most people's interior state.' So, to repeat once again – because the point needs driving home – listen to your body and your nervous system and STOP on your amber light. Do not wait for the red light. That will be too late.

But perhaps you cannot just stop to order. You still remain tense when you *do* stop, in fact possibly more tense, because you are worrying about all the things you should be doing. In which case, you need not only to stop, but deliberately to relax. This is where relaxation exercises come in. I read a book called *Simple Relaxation – the physiological method for easing tension*, by Laura Mitchell (see book list on p. 101). The method is deliberately to tense the muscles and then stop and let them relax. Shortly after reading the book I met the professor of physiology at one of the London teaching hospitals and I asked him whether he knew of the book and whether he thought it was any good. His reply was, 'It ought to be. She was one of my students'!

What about tranquillizers? I know that they are under a cloud just at present, that there is the fear of addiction, and so on. I can only speak from experience and I must say that I have known many people who have been helped by them. They are not, of course, a cure for tension. But they do damp it down. Perhaps they are 'crisis things' and should only be taken in such circumstances. Nor should we become overdependent on them; but take them only when we really need them. You can get them only on a doctor's prescription – so go to your GP, share your tension problem with him and take his advice. But if you do decide to take tranquillizers, please do not get a guilt complex about this or write yourself off as a weakling. Be positive and accept them gratefully. In fact, thank God for them. They are a useful crutch. But you do not want – and you should not need – to walk on crutches all your life. This is what I mean by 'crisis things' – little helps and aids to coping, at certain times and in certain situations.

Again – and especially if we are plagued by irrational fears, such as the fear of blame or the fear of incapacity – we need to build up our faith in God, brick by brick: our faith in his love for us and in his power to uphold us and use us. Remember, it is God who is doing the work. We are simply his instruments, his tools. However busy we are, we should never neglect or cut down our times of prayer. For it is through those times of prayer each day that we are open to God's love and power. And through that open door pour in faith and hope and love, affecting our whole life and thought and relationships. Moreover, prayer is not confined to our set times each day. Our whole day should be punctuated with little snatches of prayer. For example, before seeing each person you have to see, doing each thing you have to do, say to God: 'Lord, use me.' And when the person has gone and you have finished what you had to do, say to God: 'Thank you, Lord, for using me.' Say it in faith, however the thing *seems* to have gone, because – remember – you are not a good judge of your own performance. You are too subjective, too close to it and often very shortsighted. Hand the thing over to God and leave it with him – 'Father, into thy hands'. Then you get on with the next job in hand.

These are some of the ways and means of coping with tension, preventing it from dominating and crippling our life. But having said all this, we still have to live with our tension, as we have to live with our irrational fears, doing the best we can, as the people we are, in the circumstances which exist.

According to St John's Gospel, Jesus said to the apostles: 'You did not choose me, but I chose you.' 'I chose *you*' – a person, a particular person, with a particular sort of temperament and a particular type of personality. 'I chose you' – the whole of you, the tense bits as well as the calm, steady, quiet bits. And what is good enough for God incarnate should be good enough for us. So we must try to accept ourselves as we are, not as we should like to be, not as other people are. We must accept our tension as part of ourselves and learn to live with it as peacefully and sensibly as we can, knowing our limitations. That is humility. Yet trusting in the love and power of God. That is faith and hope.

# Part Two

## . . . with the Positives

5

# *Faith*

Jesus said, 'Have faith in God'. What do we mean by faith?

Faith is not knowledge. We do not know absolutely. We cannot be certain. As Gerard Hughes wrote in *God of Surprises*, 'If you are searching for a clear and precise notion of who God is, you will not find him in reading this book, and if ever you do find a neat and clear definition, you may be sure that it is false. God is mystery.' Thus faith has to live with doubt and will often be invaded by doubt. You cannot reason yourself into faith. As Pascal wrote, 'It is the heart which is aware of God and not reason. That is what faith is: God perceived intuitively by the heart, not by reason.' Faith is the response of the heart to God, whatever that means. Pascal described it as a wager. Kierkegaard described it as a leap, a jump.

Faith is not sight. We cannot see absolutely. Thus faith has to live with darkness. Fr Michael Hollings described it as like driving in a fog, being able to see only one or two cat's-eyes in front. We often have to travel in the blackout, feeling our way tentatively, one step at a time.

Faith is not security. We cannot be absolutely secure.

Thus faith has to live with anxiety and fear and is sometimes invaded by despair. Kierkegaard described it as the mid-point between despair and security.

What, then, is faith? Faith is *living* with the steady conviction that we are in the hand of God, who is both Love and Power. Faith is letting-go of our anxieties and fears, our doubt and despair. It is 'abandonment to divine providence' – the title of de Caussade's spiritual classic. Faith is jumping in, launching out, having a go, 'not clinging to a rock but swimming with forty thousand fathoms underneath', as Kierkegaard put it. Dietrich Bonhoeffer, writing from a Nazi prison, described it as '. . . taking life in one's stride, with all its duties and problems, its successes and failures, its experiences and helplessness. It is in such a life that we throw ourselves utterly into the arms of God . . . That is faith.'

People often say 'I wish I had faith . . . I would give anything to have faith' – as though faith were something you were born with, like having red hair or a placid temperament. But faith is something you *do*. It is a gamble you risk, a jump you take, a commitment you embrace, a choice you make, a personal trust you give. We are doing it all the time in human life. You cannot live without faith. We trust the doctor, the surgeon, the bank manager, the bus driver, the airline pilot. We trust our friends, our husband, our wife, our children.

But you cannot trust to order. And you cannot trust the obviously untrustworthy: a shady financier, a crook, a charlatan, someone who strikes you as being a bit shady, a bit devious. We trust in response to a sense of trustworthiness, a sense of integrity. Or, to put it more grandly, to an intuition or vision or experience of beauty, truth and goodness. It is this which sparks off our faith.

Christian faith is our response to the love and power of God revealed in Christ. Christians believe that God who is Mystery, the God of Surprises, has been revealed in the life and death and resurrection of Jesus. His life demonstrated the love of God, through his teaching, his healing and his warm acceptance of all sorts and conditions of people, many of whom were regarded as disreputable outcasts. His death revealed that the love of God is unbreakable. Jesus was rejected by men, tried on a trumped-up charge, handed over to the Roman authority as a danger to law and order. He was tortured and mocked and finally crucified, the victim of religious and state persecution and fear. Yet on the cross he prayed as he had lived. 'Father, forgive them, for they know not what they do.' They could do all these things to him, but they could not break his love.

His resurrection demonstrated that the power of God is unconquerable. 'Early, when it was yet dark', the early Christians experienced Christ as alive, the victor over both sin and death. In Dorothy L. Sayers's famous phrase: 'They had seen the strong hands of God take the crown of thorns and twist it into a crown of glory and in hands as strong as that they knew themselves safe.' As St Paul put it, expressing his own resurrection experience from shipwreck, perils, persecution, misunderstanding, anxiety: 'All things work together for good to them that love God.' God has the power to bring good out of the worst that evil can do. 'Who shall separate us from the love of Christ? Shall tribulation, or distress, or persecution, or famine, or peril, or sword? . . . No, in all these things we are more than conquerors through him who loved us.'

Christian faith is living our lives with the steady conviction that we are in the hand of God revealed in Christ.


'The apostles said to the Lord, "Increase our faith".' How do we grow in faith?

*We grow in faith by breathing in the love and power of God.*

We do this through our times of prayer. We open the windows of our lives and let in the fresh, clean, healing air of his grace. His grace (his gracious influence) flows into us through our prayer, bible-reading, spiritual reading, and through being quiet and still before God, sunbathing in his love and power, and through our receiving Holy Communion, the sacrament of his presence and life.

The love and power of God. 'Think on these things.' Brood on them. 'Chew' them until, bit by bit, they seep through and seep down into the very depth of our unconscious memory, where all our anxieties and fears and self-doubts lie. 'Read, mark, learn and inwardly digest' them.

*We grow in faith by deliberately injecting into our system positive, creative faith-thoughts.*

As I said in Chapter 1, on irrational fears, if we are the victims of fear, self-doubt and insecurity, a negative, cold tap will drip incessantly from our unconscious memory: I'm not . . . I can't . . . It won't . . . We need, therefore, to turn on another tap, the positive, warm tap of faith and trust. God is . . . God can . . . God will . . .

It is a good thing to have on the tip of our tongue certain faith-phrases and to swallow them like medicine – first thing in a morning, last thing at night and at odd times during the day. For example:

I *am* important to God, I *am* of value to God.
I *am* accepted by God, I *am* loved by God.
I *am* forgiven by God, here and now, just as I am.
I *can* do all things through Christ who strengthens
    me.
The eternal God *is* my refuge and underneath *are*
    the everlasting arms.

In my earlier book, *Learning to Pray*, I quoted Christopher Isherwood on the value and use of the mantra. In his study of the Hindu mystic, Ramakrishna (*Ramakrishna and his Disciples*), Isherwood wrote:

We are creatures of reverie, not of reason. We spend a very small proportion of our time thinking logical, consecutive thoughts. It is within the reverie that our passions and prejudices – often so terrible in their consequences – build themselves up, almost unnoticed, out of slogans, newspaper headlines, chance-heard words of fear and greed and hate, which have slipped into our consciousness through our unguarded eyes and ears. Our reverie expresses what we are, at any given moment. The mantra, by introducing God into the reverie, must produce profound subliminal changes. These may not be apparent for some time, but, sooner or later, they will inevitably appear – first in the prevailing mood and disposition of the individual; then in a gradual change of character.

The Hindu use of the mantra is very like the Christian use of the Jesus Prayer in meditation or ejaculatory prayer, 'arrow-prayers'.

*We grow in faith by making little experiments in faith.*
For example, handing over to God some worry and anxiety and then refusing to entertain it – or rather, *trying* not to entertain it – because we have put it into his hands. And when it comes back into our minds, back to God it must go, over and over again.

Or, setting our will to do something which we are afraid of doing, taking on something which we shirk attempting, because in spite of our fear and self-doubt, we believe that God is with us and within us and that he will use us and see us through.

Or, vice versa, refusing to take on something we are asked to do because we already have enough on our plate, being brave enough to say 'No'.

*We grow in faith by trying to live in the here and now.*
Jean-Pierre de Caussade's advice again: that we should leave the past to the mercy of God and the future to his providence and try to concentrate wholly upon 'the sacrament of the present moment'. We should try to attend to what we are doing, to the person we are talking to, to what is going on around us, instead of frittering away our energy in anxiety about the past or the future.

*We grow in faith by thanksgiving.*

'Count your blessings, count them one by one.' Look back over the past day, the past week, the past month, the past year and see how God *has* in fact upheld you, guided you, taught you, rescued you, strengthened you, brought you through, used you. Collect a list of your thanksgivings each week and throw them gratefully into the great stream of thanksgiving which flows up to God in the Eucharist.

Each thanksgiving for blessings received, each example of faith working, acts as a springboard for the next leap of faith. In the words of Cardinal Newman's famous hymn:

So long thy power hath blest me, sure it still
Will lead me on
O'er moor and fen, o'er crag and torrent, till
The night is gone.

*We grow in faith by trying to resist the enemies of faith.*

By the enemies of faith, I mean those negative thoughts and feelings of inadequacy, anxiety, fear, insecurity, despair; and irrational thoughts and feelings of guilt, of being worthless, of being unloved and unlovable. We cannot prevent these thoughts from coming into our mind, but we need not entertain them. They are a denial of the love and power of God. They should be treated as temptations and resisted, like any other temptation, the moment we are aware of them. And this we have to do over and over again, because, to quote W. H. Auden:

Then back they come
The fears that we fear. We fall asleep

Only to meet the idiot children of
Our revels and wrongs.

*We grow in faith by perseverance.*
Hanging on, in the cold and the dark, in the silence
and the storm. Going on, refusing to give up, refusing
to let go. As Archbishop Michael Ramsey wrote: 'Faith
is not security away from darkness; it is the will to go
on with darkness all around.'

Let nothing disturb thee
Nothing affright thee;
All things are passing,
God never changeth;
Patient endurance
Attaineth to all things;
Who God possesseth
In nothing is wanting;
Alone God sufficeth.

St Teresa's Bookmark

'Have faith in God.'
'Lord, increase our faith.'

# 6

## *Hope*

The atheist philosopher Feuerbach described hope as 'faith in relation to the future'.

Here are some well-known lines about hope:

'Blue skies around the corner . . .'

'It's a lovely day tomorrow, Tomorrow is a lovely day . . .'

'Someday I'll find you, Moonbeams behind you . . .'

'One day he'll come along, The man I love. And he'll be big and strong, The man I love . . .'

'They shall not hurt or destroy in all my holy mountain; for the earth shall be full of the knowledge of the Lord, as the waters cover the sea.'

'I saw a new heaven and a new earth . . . and the sea [that dividing and devouring monster] will be no more.'

'God will wipe away every tear from their eyes, and death shall be no more, neither shall there be mourning nor crying nor pain any more.'

I have deliberately mixed up secular hope and religious hope: secular hope as it was expressed in the popular songs of my youth; religious hope as it is expressed in the Bible, both in the Old Testament and (particularly) in the New Testament.

Hope appears to be a universal instinct. It is an old tree, with deep roots, which cannot be uprooted however violently the winds may blow. Over and over again in history, when reason would have assumed that people would collapse, fall apart, under successive blows of disappointment, disaster, suffering, oppression, persecution and death, they did not in fact collapse, fall apart. They somehow went on. And they went on hoping – for relief, release, liberation.

In fact, it was hope which kept them going. Victims of an unhappy marriage. Victims of bereavement. Prisoners in jail with long sentences. Prisoners of conscience. People in hospital awaiting an operation. People frustrated in their work. Or – much worse – people unable to find work. Oppressed and often persecuted minorities. Social reformers, campaigning against injustice, inequality and discrimination. Scientists and research workers, seeking to discover hidden factors and the causes of disease. Artists, trying to express beauty in word or sound or colour.

Such people live in hope. They hope against all hope. They hope that, one day, their marriage will come right; that heaven is a reality, not a fantasy; that, one day, those prison gates will open and they will be free; that the operation will be successful; that, one day, they will uncover the factors they are looking for and discover the causes of cancer; that they will be able to express their vision of beauty adequately.

As John Macquarrie wrote in his book of Christian meditations, *The Humility of God*, 'So it has been from the beginning, for although the shadow of evil and death has fallen over every life, it has been met by hope and belief in a promise of better things.'

In the fourteenth century there was a woman called Julian who lived on her own in Norwich. In the course of a very severe illness, which appeared to be fatal, she experienced a number of 'revelations' or 'showings' of God.

At one point during her suffering, she wrestled – as all believers in God have to wrestle – with the problem of evil. What price God, whose nature and being is love, in a world which is so full of suffering, oppression, evil and death? How can you square belief in God with the fact of evil? It presents an impossible, insoluble paradox.

Then there came to her this 'revelation' of God. Julian seemed to hear God saying to her '. . . but all shall be well, and all shall be well, and all manner of thing shall be well'.

She meditated on these words and, years later, when she had quite recovered from her illness, she wrote a book which has become a spiritual classic. It is called *Revelations of Divine Love*. I shall quote a few sentences:

And so our good Lord answered to all the questions and doubts which I could raise, saying most comfortingly: 'I may make all things well, and I can make all things well, and I shall make all things well; and you will see yourself that every kind of thing will be well . . .' And in these words God wishes us to be enclosed in rest and peace . . . For just as the blessed Trinity created all things from nothing; just so will the same blessed Trinity make everything well which is not well . . . it seemed to me that it was impossible that every kind of thing should be well . . . And to this I had no other answer . . . except this: 'What is impossible to you is not impossible to me . . . I shall make everything well.'

To live with this faith that ultimately 'all shall be well' is to live in hope. Hope is 'faith in relation to the future'.

Now we may not be among that list of people I itemized earlier, those who live in apparently hopeless situations and yet hope against all hope. Our marriage may not be unhappy, we may not have suffered a close bereavement, we may not be in prison or in hospital. We may not belong to a minority group. We may be neither scientists nor artists. Nevertheless, we all need to practise the virtue of hope. As with faith, we cannot really live positively without hope.

Hope is a religious virtue, as well as a human instinct. The neo-Marxist Ernst Bloch wrote: 'Where there is hope, there is religion.' Hope is believing that the power of God will ultimately achieve his purpose. His purpose is love. So hope is believing that love will ultimately prevail and triumph.

The Christian ground of that hope is the resurrection of Christ. As the First Letter of Peter says, 'Blessed be the God and Father of our Lord Jesus Christ! By his great mercy we have been born anew to a living hope through the resurrection of Jesus Christ from the dead.'

But if hope is a virtue, then despair is a sin. I do not mean, of course, the despair which is a symptom of clinical depression. I mean the despair which is a refusal to believe that God has the power to achieve his purpose. This is a denial of the resurrection. Such despair issues in pessimism and cynicism. The worst has happened in the worst of all possible worlds! 'Eat, drink and be merry, for tomorrow we die.' Hope, on the other hand, gives us a sense of expectancy, the ability to look forward and to keep going, the will never to give up.

But it is not easy to practise the virtue of hope. No virtue is easy. Otherwise it would not be called a virtue. We often feel trapped in a dark tunnel, unable to move backwards or forwards. We are rooted to the spot in terror and immobility. This is the moment of temptation: the temptation to despair, to pack it in, to give up believing and hoping. To practise the virtue of hope in this sort of situation is to see-without-seeing a small chink of light at the end of the long, cold, dark tunnel and to walk gingerly but steadily towards it.

Hope is not naive, romantic optimism which simply has not faced the enormity, the length and depth and breadth of evil. Hope is not whistling in the dark. As John Macquarrie wrote, 'Hope is rather the faith that when man falls and even when the worst evils happen in this ambiguous world, we never find ourselves at the end of the road. The Creator God is ahead of us, waiting to open up a new possibility.' The disciples hoped in Christ. But then came the crucifixion and they slunk away in despair and fear, all hope abandoned. But then came the resurrection and the birth of a new hope which enabled them and their successors to endure persecution for centuries.

To quote from Julian of Norwich again:

'You will not be overcome' . . . And these words, 'You will not be overcome', were said very insistently and strongly, for certainty and strength against every tribulation which may come. He did not say, 'You will not be troubled, you will not be belaboured, you will not be disquieted', but he said, 'You will not be overcome'. God wants us to pay attention to these words and always to be strong in faithful trust, in well-being and in woe . . . and all shall be well.

But it will not *feel* well. If it *felt* well, if we could *see* light at the end of the dark tunnel, hope would not be hope. Hope is hanging on, moving on, going on through the darkness and the cold, hoping as it were against all hope.

I can well understand black South Africans today losing hope in the possibility of a peaceful solution to their problems and turning, in despair, to violence. We certainly have no right to blame them. It was as long ago as 1956 that Bishop Trevor Huddleston wrote *Naught for your Comfort*, warning us of what would happen in South Africa if the world community did nothing about it. We did not heed that warning.

There was a profile of Allan Boesak, one of the black leaders in South Africa, in *The Times* recently. He agonizes over the morality of violence and can find no good argument against Calvin's concept of 'public avengers' raised up by God 'to punish unrighteous domination'. Yet he sees that this is not how the power of God will achieve the triumph of love. Thus he says: 'I really don't believe that violence can ultimately solve problems. I am desperately afraid of what violence does to people, the soul-destroying element of violence, the ease with which one slips into using violence, and the difficulty of breaking a cycle of violence once it has begun.' There is a man in a dark tunnel, unable to see which way to go and yet dreading the violence of despair, endeavouring to hang on to hope. He and so many like him badly need and deserve our prayers.

When we read in Julian of Norwich, '. . . and all shall be well, and all shall be well, and all manner of thing shall be well', that is not a recipe for us to sit back and do nothing but simply wait for God to 'make all things well'. That would be to turn religion into pure escapism. No! We have our part to play, our work to do to 'make all things well'. For, as St Paul wrote to the Christians in Corinth, we are – or should be – 'workers together with him'.

When God created us with the power of free will, he limited himself. He put himself, to some extent, into our hands. Such is the humility of God. We depend upon him utterly. Indeed we do. But, to some extent, he also depends upon us. He depends upon our willing, active co-operation. We have our little bit to do, by the grace of God, to 'make all things well': in personal relationships; in social relationships; in racial relationships; in national relationships; in respect for the environment. There are all sorts of ways and means of making our voice heard and our influence felt. We must never despair of the power of personal influence. Christ calls us to be lights in the world, pinches of salt in the earth.

'God is working his purpose out as year succeeds to year', we sing in a hymn. Indeed he is. That is our faith and the ground of our hope for the future. But the third verse of that hymn asks:

What can we do to work God's work, to prosper
    and increase
The brotherhood of all mankind, the reign of the
    Prince of Peace?
What can we do to hasten the time, the time that
    shall surely be,
When the earth shall be filled with the glory of God
    as the waters cover the sea.

What can *we* do?

So the virtue of hope is not only a consolation, an assurance of the ultimate victory of God over evil. It is also an inspiration, a challenge, a responsibility. We are to live in hope, to think and feel and *act* hopefully as 'workers together with him'.


How, you might ask, do we grow in hope? The same way that we grow in faith, since hope is 'faith in relation to the future'. By meditating on the power of God, his ability to bring good out of evil. By trying always to look on the bright side. By saying to yourself, when you are under a cloud of pain or disappointment or fear, 'This will lift'. By refusing to give way to despair. By trying to live each day in hope. That is how an American Presbyterian minister, who was taken hostage, described how he managed to live through his ordeal of many weeks and months. There is a poem by Charles Péguy called 'The bud of hope'. I shall quote one line: 'Hope wakes up every morning, and goes to sleep every night, and sleeps very well.'

Hope is expressed by patience and perseverance. It also leads to joy. Pope John Paul, preaching in Harlem in 1979, said: 'I bring you news of great joy, joy to be shared by all people. Many people never feel joy. Instead, they tread the path of despair. They live in our neighbourhoods, they walk down our streets, they may even be members of our own family; but they live without joy, because they live without hope. We are the Easter people and Alleluia is our song.'

7

## *Love*

St Paul described love as the greatest of the virtues, greater than faith, greater than hope, the most positive thing in life.

We are certainly made for love. We are made to love and to be loved, and if we are robbed of love we wither and die like a plant without water. We become embittered and resentful, envious and jealous, cold and hard, withdrawn and defensive or pugnacious and aggressive. A person without love turns to hate, hatred of himself, hatred of other people, hatred of society. And if you think that I am being too dramatic, too extreme, at least you will agree that a person robbed of love will not achieve his or her potential. There will be something stunted about them.

To rob a person of love is to rob them of God, since 'God is Love'. God's love is often mediated, experienced, not so much directly as through other people; which is perhaps why, when two people 'fall in love', they feel that there is something 'out of this world' about it, something transcendent, divine. Or why we take our cue about the love of God from the love which we received from our parents as children. And why to call God 'Father' conjures up a loving

54

image. But suppose you received no love from your parents when you were a child. Then you will not know what love is. Suppose you had a cold, hostile, disapproving, violent father. Then you will hate God, because the Father image will spell for you a negative image against which you will rebel. Such people will have to wait for the experience of love and the experience of God to be mediated to them through another person later in life. Nevertheless, such people begin life with a minus and they will always be a little anxious about love – which shows how very important our childhood is to our future development, negative or positive.

But I am rushing ahead too fast. I have not yet defined what I mean by love. It is very difficult to define this word, because it covers so much. There are different kinds of love and different areas of life to which it applies. But I must try.

Love is a yearning for, a desire for union with, another person. Love is caring for, cherishing, the beloved. It is sensitive and unselfish. It desires to give as well as to receive. It is prepared to make sacrifices. It is patient and forbearing. It tries to forgive and to go on forgiving. Love is accepting, respecting, other people as people of value, having the same value which we instinctively claim for ourselves. It pays attention to them, looks at them and listens to them. It is thoughtful and considerate, kind and generous. It is warm and welcoming. Love is a reflection of God himself. It spills out into the whole of his creation, embracing not only particular people but what we call society, the community in which we live, the world itself which has become more and more a global village.

It includes the earth on which we depend. And of course it embraces God, the Lord of creation, the Author and Giver of life, the Maker of heaven and earth.


'You shall love the Lord your God with all your heart, and with all your soul, and with all your mind, and with all your strength.'

We are to love God with the whole of us, to live our life for the glory of God. Duke Ellington, the jazz musician, was once asked by a rather cynical reporter why he went on into old age composing music and conducting concerts. 'Why do you do it, Duke? I guess it's the dough, isn't it?' Ellington replied, 'No, man, I reckon I do it for the glory of God.' In a Christian discussion group somewhere in France during the war, the question came up: 'What is the duty of a Christian lorry driver?' A number of pious suggestions were made. Then a bright spark, sitting at the back, got up and said: 'The job of a Christian lorry driver is to drive a lorry and to glorify God by driving it well.' End of discussion!

Our love of God is in response to his love for us, revealed once and for all in the life and death and resurrection of Christ. 'We love because he first loved us.' It is expressed in our prayer, giving time to God, paying attention to him, seeking to communicate with him, to be united with him. It is expressed in trying to live in faith and hope. It is expressed in our desire to co-operate with God, endeavouring to do his will and to act according to his ways. It is expressed in a desire to reflect his love in our lives and our relationships. It is expressed in respect and love for the whole of his creation.

'You shall love your neighbour as yourself.'

Our neighbour is God's other child, as much valued, accepted, loved and forgiven by God as we are. As Père Grou, a French spiritual director, wrote in the eighteenth century: 'As in the word "Father" is contained every motive for loving God, so in the words "Our Father" are reasons for loving our neighbour.'

Moreover, in loving our neighbour, we are loving Christ. When St Paul had his mystical experience on the Damascus road, he seemed to hear Christ saying to him: 'Saul, Saul, why do you persecute me?' Paul had not been persecuting Christ. He had been persecuting certain Christian men and women who believed and preached that Christ had risen from the dead. But the words were unmistakable: 'Why do you persecute *me*?' So Christ was somehow *in* those men and women whom Paul had been persecuting. Again, at the end of his parable of the sheep and the goats, Jesus said, 'As you did it [or did not do it] to one of the least of these my brothers, you did it [or did not do it] to *me*.' Did – or did not do – what? Gave drink to the thirsty, welcomed the stranger, clothed the naked, visited the sick, cared for the prisoner. By caring and attending to *them* in their various needs, they were caring and attending to Christ. That gives an immense importance, a transcendent mystery, to every single person we meet. Whatever they look like, however they behave, whatever they have done, whether we like them or dislike them, are attracted to them or repelled by them, nevertheless, hidden under their outward appearance there is Christ himself, if only we have eyes to see. It is this thought, this vision, which inspired the saints all down the ages to care for lepers, live with the poor, befriend prisoners, pick up destitutes. They were caring for, living with, befriending, rescuing from the gutter, Christ himself. Mother Teresa, describing the work of her community in caring for the destitute and the dying in Calcutta, said: 'Our work calls for us to see Jesus in everyone. He has told us that he is the hungry one. He is the naked one. He is the thirsty one. He is the one without a home. He is the one who is suffering. These are our treasures. They are Jesus. Each one is Jesus in his distressing disguise.' That is a phrase we might well remember, whenever we see a down-and-out, a meths drinker, a young man or woman 'high' on drugs, a person suffering from AIDS: 'Jesus in his distressing disguise'.

But Jesus does not always appear in a 'distressing disguise'. He sometimes appears in an intimate disguise, a casual disguise, a hostile disguise, a social, political disguise, a racial disguise, an environmental disguise. Our job is to penetrate through these various disguises and to find Christ there, below the surface in our various 'neighbours'. For we have different kinds of neighbour with whom we have different kinds of relationship.

First of all, there are *our intimate relationships* with our neighbour. Our marriage, our family, our close friendships.

I think that we need to cultivate these intimate

relationships, never to take them for granted, never to 'settle down'. Rather, we should explore and go on exploring, discover and go on discovering, the mystery of the other person.

We should never seek to possess, to dominate and manipulate the other person. Nor should we be over-dependent upon him or her. That would be to turn them into idols, to treat them as God, whereas they are imperfect human beings, as we are, with their own limitations, vulnerabilities and fears.

You cannot, of course, avoid hurting or being hurt by those you love. As a popular song of the 1930s put it:

You always hurt the one you love,
The one you shouldn't hurt at all.

And if you are hurt, you will inevitably react, either by withdrawing into yourself or by becoming aggressive, according to temperament. But, instead of wallowing in jealousy, for example, or fear or resentment or self-pity, we should try to move on, as quickly as possible, to the second reaction, which is that of faith and love, understanding and forgiveness. And if *you* have done the hurting, then quickly apologize and make up.

Above all, these intimate relationships are to be enjoyed. They are gifts of God, for which we should always be thankful. They are one of the great joys of human life.

In our friendships, of course, we inevitably become separated by space and time. But we can still keep in touch by writing letters. Some people are very good at this and their letters are so much 'them' that we can almost see them and hear them talking. And yet paradoxically – such is their mystery – these intimate relationships are unaffected by space and time. And when we *do* meet up again, it is as though it were yesterday or last week!


Then there are *our casual relationships*.

Relationships with the neighbours next door or across the road. Colleagues at work. The butcher, the baker, the hairdresser, the assistants in the grocer's shop or the supermarket where we go regularly. The people we meet casually in the street, on the Underground or in the bus. Other parents we meet as we wait to collect the children. People we meet in church, in a group, at a committee meeting. Anywhere and everywhere, we have our casual relationships.

Such people are not a Thou, like our husband, our wife, our children, our friends. We cannot have the same degree of intimacy with them. But they are a You. They are persons, each one a He, a She – never an It. As David Jenkins wrote in *The Contradiction of Christianity*, '. . . human beings are not things, they are persons. And in the Christian vision and understanding they are not just historical persons . . . they are potentially eternal persons.' They are persons of value, having precisely the same value which we claim for ourselves. As Jesus said, 'And as you would that men should do to you, do you also to them likewise'. It makes such a difference to people how they are treated. It can make the sun come out or the rain to fall. It makes us grow in value or diminish.

Then there are *our threatening, hostile relationships*.

There are people who somehow 'get on our nerves'. People we 'can't stand'. People who make us feel awkward and shy. People who make us feel inferior. People we are afraid of.

There is a chemistry between people. One person attracts me, while another repels. Some people trigger off my vulnerabilities, awaken unconscious memories of buried hurts and fears. What to do about that? There is nothing much you *can* do directly. You just have to learn to live with it as best you can. Baron von Hügel in *Spiritual Counsels and Letters* has some wise words to say about what he calls our 'antipathies':

> The wise way to fight antipathies is *never* to fight them directly – turn gently to other sights, images, thoughts etc. If it – the hate – persists, bear it gently like a fever or a toothache – do not speak to it – better not to speak of it even to God . . . It is an itch – scratching makes it worse . . . I know too that you should never strain, never directly strive to like people. Just merely drop or ignore your antipathies . . . to keep quietly ignoring all that rumpus – that is all that God asks, and we then grow, through, and on occasion of, these involuntary vehemencies.

But, although they may threaten us and although we may feel hostile towards them, these people are still persons. They probably have their own problems to cope with, their own vulnerabilities. Perhaps their (to us) threatening and hostile appearance may be a mask behind which they hide their own anxieties, fears and inferiorities. We cannot avoid reacting to them as we do, but we should try not to let our subjective reaction blind and deafen us to the fact that they are persons with all the mystery of a human person. And, so far as we can, we should try to treat them as persons, neither running away from them nor looking down our noses at them.

Moreover, we cannot avoid the challenge of Jesus. 'Love your enemies, do good to those who hate you, bless those who curse you, pray for those who abuse you.' This almost supernatural attitude can perhaps only come as the result of our prayer, our communion with God, through which his grace flows into us, enabling us to be and to do what we could not be or do in our own sinful, self-centred, human nature.


Then there are *our pastoral relationships* with other people.

You may well say, 'I'm not a priest, a minister, a deacon – I haven't got any pastoral relationships!' Oh yes you have – or you will have. If you are an understanding, caring person, other people will notice. And they will turn to you with their problems, share with you their difficulties, anxieties and sorrows. 'But I am not trained!' you say. You do not have to be. In their preface to *Disordered Lives* Douglas Hooper and John Roberts, both Lecturers in Mental Health in the University of Bristol, wrote: '. . . the expert training largely consists of experience in handling problems . . . In fact, most people are already well on the way to helping others satisfactorily when they are sympathetic, patient, interested and mature in their bearing towards them.' So there!

But what can we do? We can listen. The healing power of sheer listening cannot be overestimated.

When you listen to another person objectively, giving him or her the whole of your attention, that in itself gives value to a person, or restores value if, for example, they have been robbed of it by rejection. I read a psychiatric textbook some years ago, by Stafford-Clark, called *Psychiatry for Students*. He described the framework for a psychotherapy interview. Seventy per cent of the time, listen and accept; twenty per cent of the time, question and interpret; ten per cent of the time, reassure and advise. I found this division of time very interesting, with its emphasis upon listening. Surely that is within our capacity. We can all listen. We can listen acceptingly, sympathetically. We can listen reassuringly, comfortingly. We can also listen intuitively, being open both to the person and to the spirit of God within us, so that we can pick up little hints and clues.

I remember watching a TV programme on 'Outsiders and Outcasts' as far back as 1966. It was about a woman called Judith Piepe. She was a German Jewess, captured by the Nazis and tortured. She wandered around Europe, a refugee without a passport. Brought up as an atheist, she later became a Christian and devoted her life to befriending young drug addicts in the clubs and cafés of Soho. The interview went like this:

Q   'You don't actually approach anybody; they approach you. Why is that?'

A   'When you have been a refugee without passport, etc., you know what it is to be an outcast. I am not an outcast now, but the scars are still there. If you have had TB, the scars are

> still visible under X-ray; and outcasts have X-ray eyes.'
> Q 'How would you try to help them?'
> A 'By making friends with them – it is always easier to help people who are your friends! And trying to break through their sense of isolation.'

She went on: 'Some poisonous advice is often given to people who are training to do social work – don't get involved. That is nonsense. You have to get involved. The priest who trained me for this work said "If you want to help people, you have to love them. Otherwise they will never forgive you for the bread you give them." As a Christian, you have to be involved. That is the meaning of the incarnation.'

Then there are *our social, political relationships*.

Sociology shows us the influence of social, cultural conditioning. Thus, love is not just a matter of caring for individuals. It also involves being concerned about social policies and structures. As David Jenkins has written, '. . . we are now alerted, as never before, to the immense effects on human living, both individual and corporate, of social, economic and political relationships . . . A love which denies all attention to politics would seem to lose credibility, as refusing to pay attention to that which causes so many to suffer' (*The Contradiction of Christianity*).

We have a vision of human beings as made in the image of God, indwelt by the living Christ, temples of the Holy Spirit. We need, therefore, to ask the question: how is this policy, this economic programme, this social structure, going to affect people? Is it going to benefit them, especially the more needy, or to deprive them? Is it going to give them more personal value or less? And we have to give or withhold our support, to cast our vote, accordingly.

One thing is very obvious. We can have nothing to do with racism. Racism values or devalues persons according to the colour of their skin. This is not only irrational, it is immoral. It is a denial of God's creation. Any policy or programme which is racist must be strongly opposed. And the same is true of sexism, valuing or devaluing a person according to his or her sex.


Finally, there are *our environmental relationships*, our love for God's creation.

Angelo of Foligno, an Umbrian mystic of the thirteenth century, who after her husband's death became a Franciscan tertiary, used to say 'The world is full of God'. Teilhard de Chardin said the same thing in *Le Milieu divin*: 'To repeat: by virtue of the creation and, still more, of the incarnation, nothing here below is profane for those who know how to see . . . By means of all created things, without exception, the divine assails us, penetrates us and moulds us.'

The Holy Spirit is active in creation. He is the Life within all life, throbbing through life like a hidden dynamo. 'God so loved the world' that he came into the world and shared its life as one of us. The incarnate Christ said 'Consider [look at] the birds of the air . . . the lilies of the field'.

To love God's creation is to enjoy it: simply to look

in wonder at flowers and trees and hills and rivers, using all our senses of sight and hearing, touch and smell.

> A poor life this if, full of care,
> We have no time to stand and stare.
>                                    W. H. Davies

But we also have a responsibility for creation. This should lead us to oppose the things which disfigure it – manmade ugliness in all its forms: great tower blocks which destroy the skyline and deface our cities; the spoliation of natural beauty for material ends and in the interest of quick profits. We shall join hands with the conservationists here.

We shall be opposed to the use of nuclear weapons and their escalation in the competitive arms race. For these weapons threaten and could so easily *destroy* creation.

We cannot just sit back and let these things happen. For we are God's stewards in creation and one day we shall have to give an account of our stewardship.

What can we do? Look around and think about it. There are many groups of people who are protesting against these things. Ought we to join them? And if so, which group? Over and over again in history, it has been shown that small pressure groups *can* achieve things. As Bob Geldof said in Hyde Park at the beginning of 'The Race against Time' campaign, 'We are able to change the world we live in'. So we should not despair and feel helpless and hopeless.

Love does not mean the absence of conflict: conflict

within ourselves (between faith and fear, for example), conflict with other people, conflict in society. To pretend that love involves the absence of conflict is to castrate love, to make it unreal, mere sentimental treacle. Conflict is inevitable in human life. Wherever there is difference – a difference of temperament, or sex, opinion, culture and life-style, ideals and values, interests – there is bound to be conflict. And so inevitably we find conflict all around us: personal, marital, sexual, social, racial, political, economic, national, ideological. Love cannot keep out of conflict without retreating from life altogether. In fact, love often drives us into conflict. The mistake we make is to assume that conflict is always destructive. But this need not be so. Conflict can also be constructive. It is the attitude we bring to it which often makes it either destructive or constructive.

Conflict inevitably becomes destructive if we come to it with the infallible conviction of our own rightness: 'Am I right or am I right?' to quote Dennis Potter in *The Singing Detective*. But this is the sin of pride. This is closed-mindedness. There is no possibility of dialogue, of understanding and learning. It is a battle of cops and robbers, goodies and baddies. We should always come to a conflict situation with humility, realizing that we are fallible human beings, incapable of grasping the whole truth. Moreover, we are conditioned, prejudiced human beings, with a particular social and cultural background, a particular set of values. We have our blindspots. We are also imperfect, sinful human beings, unable to 'throw the first stone'. If we remember this, then there is a possibility that the conflict may become constructive.

Conflict is also likely to be destructive if we bring to it our fears and vulnerabilities: our fear of blame and violence, for instance, our fear of incapacity and failure, or our fear of insecurity. We shall then be too much on our guard, too anxious to maintain our position. We shall approach the conflict too subjectively, anxious about our reputation. We shall not be objective, free to be open to the other person. We shall feel threatened, unable to say what we mean, to show what we feel; and we may well get our sums wrong. We should always approach a conflict situation with faith: the belief that we are in God's hands and that he will use us. We should deliberately say 'Lord, use me', and then try to let ourselves go and concentrate our attention wholly upon what is being said, what is going on, from moment to moment. Then again, there is a possibility that the conflict may become constructive.

Where does love come in? Love is allied to humility and faith. But it has its own contribution to make as well. Love will affect our attitude and the way we behave in a conflict situation. However much we may dislike our 'opponent', however much we may hate his or her views, however violently we may disagree with their interpretation of the situation, nevertheless, love reminds us that he or she is a person of value, equally loved by God, and it is required of us to treat them accordingly. This will involve the conquering of personal hatred and the desire to hurt; the avoidance of contempt and the despising look; the attempt merely to score points. Love requires us to respect the other person as a person: to be open to him or to her, to look and to listen; to try to understand. Love will also endeavour to bring humour into the situation, to defuse the heat of argument. Love will be honest and straightforward, neither twofaced nor devious. Nor will it allow itself to be manipulated. It will not be a doormat to be walked over. It will fight for the right as it sees it, but not with dirty tricks. It will not try to get its own way at all costs. It will be prepared to give, to concede. It will desire, if possible, to reconcile the differences, to find a constructive solution.

'Love is always patient and kind; it is never jealous; love is never boastful or conceited; it is never rude or selfish; it does not take offence, and is not resentful. Love takes no pleasure in other people's sins but delights in the truth; it is always ready to excuse, to trust, to hope, and to endure whatever comes. Love does not come to an end' (1 Corinthians 13:4–8. The Jerusalem Bible).

'In the eventide of our life, we shall be judged on love' (St John of the Cross).

*8*

## *Gratitude*

We once had staying with us an old lady who was a shining example of this virtue of gratitude, this very positive attitude to life. She was over eighty and lived on her own in South London, not far from Wandsworth prison. The police were frequent visitors to her particular road: in the cellar of one house, £5 notes were successfully forged for many years; a room in another house was used as a brothel; racial tension reared its ugly head from time to time. Such was her environment. She had just recovered from a bad attack of shingles which had affected her eyes. Yet she was a person of immense vitality. She loved the theatre and the bright lights. She was fascinated by people and places. She had an insatiable interest in all that was going on. That summer, she had climbed a mountain in the Lake District. Somehow, she had kept a childlike sense of wonder and excitement and an intense enjoyment of life. She often said 'I keep pinching myself. Isn't it marvellous to be alive!'

I do not know how she prayed, what she did in her prayer time, but I should imagine that she spent most of the time saying 'Thank you' to God. I know that she went to Communion each week and again I imagine

70

that for her the Holy Communion meant above all the Eucharist, the Great Thanksgiving, offered by the people of God to the Author and Giver of Life.

Do *you* think it is marvellous to be alive? How much space and time does thanksgiving occupy in your prayers? How much space and time does self-pity take up in your thoughts? How much space and time does grumbling occupy in your conversation? I think all these personal questions hang together, an association of ideas. One thing leads to another.

It is not easy these days to keep a sense of wonder and excitement and an enjoyment of life. So often, life is one long rush, a rat race, a battle against time, a neurotic nightmare in which you have to pack a suitcase and try to catch a train which is not going to wait. Things keep falling out and the lock will not fasten. Overpressure dulls our sensitivity. We do not notice things. 'We have no time to stand and stare.' And so we lose our sense of wonder.

Moreover, life today is lived under the shadow of grim newspaper headlines and horrific television pictures. We are more aware than ever before of pain, tragedy and evil on a global scale. Disaster, suffering, violence, crime and squalor: we are bombarded with these. The bombardment is good if it quickens our sense of involvement in the world, our responsibility and our sympathy. It is a truth about life. But if it is all the truth we see, it is a distortion of the truth. For there is another side to life besides pain, tragedy and evil. There is still beauty in the world, to be seen and heard and felt. There is still goodness in the world, to be met and admired. There is still love in the world, to fill us with warmth and peace and joy.

The angels keep their ancient places –
Turn but a stone, and start a wing!
'Tis ye, 'tis your estranged faces
That miss the many-splendoured thing.
Francis Thompson

How can we keep a sense of wonder amidst all the rush and bustle? How can we cultivate sensitivity, awareness and enjoyment of life in the world today, seeing the other side, keeping things in proportion? How, in other words, can we remain *thankful* for life? I suggest that there are three moments, three opportunities for stopping to think, for consideration and reflection, for gratitude and thanksgiving.

*The first moment* is every day when we say our prayers.

Whatever our particular way of prayer, whether through words or thoughts or silence, thanksgiving should come in. And it should come in in a big way. You can overdo self-examination and confession in prayer. It can lead to unhealthy introspection and guilt. You can overdo petition. It can lead to an infantile, selfish using of God. But you cannot overdo thanksgiving. Not only is it an expression of our faith in God as the Author and Giver of Life, it is also a healing, therapeutic activity in itself. It turns us away from ourselves to God, substituting praise for pride, faith for fear, hope for despair, light for darkness.

But let us take pains with it. Do not ever let thanksgiving become a formality. Look back on the past day and pick out bits of gratitude as you would pick flowers in a garden, arranging them, smelling them, enjoying the look of them, and give glory to God for each one. Perhaps something we have learned, a new insight, a changed relationship, and so on.

*The second moment* is every week in the Eucharist.

One of the advantages of the new liturgies is that there is more thanksgiving in them than in the old service: thanksgiving for creation, for redemption (liberation) through Christ, for the life-giving Spirit.

> Lift up your hearts.
> We lift them up unto the Lord.
> Let us give thanks unto the Lord our God.
> It is meet and right so to do.

Do not let this moment come and go like something seen through the window of a railway carriage. Prepare for it the night before. Look back over the past week and pick your flowers of gratitude to bring with you. And let them be your own flowers which you have picked with your own hands from your own garden. In other words, let them be real.

Do you notice how thanksgiving rises to a crescendo, as in human love? 'Thank you for the chocolates, thank you for ironing my shirt, thank you for being nice to me, thank you for being you.' So in the Eucharist, we thank God for particular things *and then*, with angels and archangels and with all the company of heaven

> . . . we laud and magnify thy glorious name,
> evermore praising thee and saying:
> Holy, holy, holy, Lord God of Hosts,
> Heaven and earth are full of thy glory.
> Glory be to thee, O Lord most high.
>
> (Rite B. The Alternative Service Book)

*The third moment* is at odd times during the day.

Whatever the weather, circumstantially or psychologically, we all have moments sometime during the day when we are 'surprised by joy', to quote the title of C. S. Lewis's autobiography: moments when we are suddenly made aware of beauty, truth, goodness, love; moments when we are pricked alive by someone or something. Our attention is nudged by a sudden sight or sound or feeling. These are the moments when we should express our wonder and gratitude by a quick ejaculatory prayer of thanksgiving. 'Thanks be to God.' Or simply 'Glory'. Remember that old lady: 'I keep pinching myself. Isn't it marvellous to be alive!' Whenever you are aware that it is marvellous to be alive, just say so to God, giving him the glory.

But we are not always 'surprised by joy'. We are often surprised by just the opposite. By sadness, pain and suffering. By rejection, bereavement, depression and despair. Creation is not all beauty and grandeur. There is ugliness and squalor, tragedy and disaster. Is it so 'marvellous to be alive' in a world of such sharp contrasts? And when 'the slings and arrows of outrageous fortune' find their mark in our own experience – what price gratitude then?

St Paul was no stranger to creation's 'shadow-side', no stranger to suffering. In his Second Letter to the church in Corinth he wrote: 'Five times I had the thirty-nine lashes; three times I have been shipwrecked and once adrift in the open sea for a night and a day. Constantly travelling, I have been in danger from rivers and in danger from brigands, in danger from my own people and in danger from pagans; in danger in the towns, in danger in the open country, danger at sea and danger from so-called brothers. I have worked and laboured, often without sleep; I have been hungry and thirsty and often starving; I have been in the cold without clothes . . .' Yet, the same man could write in another letter that Christians should 'give thanks in all circumstances . . . for all things . . . whatever happens'.

But is such gratitude possible when we are confronted by creation's 'shadow-side'? And when pain and suffering, tragedy and disaster hit us personally? How on earth can we 'give thanks in *all* circumstances . . . for *all* things . . . *whatever* happens'?

I suppose we can thank God for the safety net, the assurance that 'underneath are the everlasting arms' – underneath everything, underneath the worst that can happen.

> And yet there's always One whose gentle hands
> This universal falling can't fall through.

Perhaps we might even go further and realize that in our suffering we are mysteriously sharing in the suffering of God. For Christ, who was the image of the Father, himself suffered, a victim on the cross of creation. So we are not alone and abandoned in our pain and suffering, tragedy and disaster. God is Emmanuel, which means God-with-us – God with us everywhere, even in our suffering, sharing it with us. And I suppose we might just be able to thank him for that.

However, there is more to be said than this. But it can only be said in faith and hope, or arise out of our own experience. Although creation has its 'shadow-side' and although God suffers in his creation, yet his love and power are not defeated, overcome, by pain and suffering, tragedy and disaster. The crucifixion was followed by the resurrection. The apparent defeat of God was followed by his victory. This is not something which happened 'once upon a time', two thousand years ago. It is happening all the time. There is a crucifixion–resurrection pattern running through the whole of life, through history and creation. It is a fact of experience that God can and God does bring good out of evil, mysteriously turning crucifixion into resurrection. As John Tinsley, formerly Bishop of Bristol, wrote: 'Dying, rising, dying, rising is the permanent rhythm of the Christian life.'

Let me tell you about a young woman I know, whose experience illustrates very vividly this crucifixion–resurrection pattern. When I first knew her she was a teenager and, like most teenagers, she was 'a bit mixed-up'. She was a very extrovert and adventurous girl. She joined the WAAF and travelled all over the world before she got married. And then – out of a blue sky, it seemed – she was stricken with very bad attacks of epilepsy. When these were eventually brought under control by means of some 'heavy' drugs, she formed a local society in her neighbourhood to help, support and befriend other epileptics. Some years passed and then one day I received this letter from her:

My dear Evan,
They say it never rains but it pours . . . I believe I wrote telling you I was having a lump removed from my vocal cords – well, I have seen the specialist again

and the lump was malignant . . . Perhaps the most wonderful and amazing thing to me about the whole situation is that I seem to have been given the gift of faith at this time . . . I have never experienced this strength of faith before in my life.

Four months later, I received another letter from her, telling me about her illness:

It is difficult to describe what it was really like, but I made a note in my diary at the time, part of which I'll quote to you – 'I feel I have experienced more pain and discomfort these past weeks than ever before. I am totally exhausted and feel that only the prayers of others and the knowledge of God have kept me going. I shall be glad when it is finished. Praise God that he has kept me going' . . . When I first came out of hospital I was only able to get about in a wheelchair, partly because I was weak and wobbly because my balance had been totally upset . . . When I couldn't do much, I bought myself a guitar and started teaching myself to play; after four months I am beginning to get quite proficient at it. In fact, when I am a bit better I'm hoping to get a group together to play some of these modern hymns and involve some of the younger children with their recorders . . .

The letter ended:

Although God never 'sends' illness, it can be used in wonderful ways and I feel that no matter how destructive a thing may be, we can always turn it into something positive and constructive. In those dark days of my illness, the only thing I could hold on to was my faith, but God used that and radiated it out to all who met me. Perhaps I shouldn't be amazed, but I am, at the effect my illness and the way I've come through it has had on people here . . .

So perhaps we *can*, after all, amazing as it may seem, 'give thanks in *all* circumstances, for *all* things, *whatever* happens'.

Moreover, as this story illustrates, our faith and gratitude in the midst of suffering can have a very positive effect on other people, making them stop and think, look and wonder.

Gratitude, however, is not only a personal, spiritual attitude and response to life, to creation, to God. It is also an attitude and response to other people.

We owe so much to other people: to our parents, our husband, our wife, our children, our friends, our teachers; to doctors, dentists, nurses, priests; to people who serve us in shops, on the train, the bus, the Underground. They may be paid to do this. Nevertheless, it is a service to us personally.

We are given so much by other people every day and all day long. Imponderable things, such as understanding, sympathy, patience, forbearance, kindness, generosity, forgiveness. Are we aware of this? Are we grateful? Or do we take it all for granted? If we do, then we are very self-centred and complacent, very ungrateful.

We are usually very sensitive to ingratitude ourselves. We do not like to be taken for granted. That is the cry of many a wife to many a husband. And vice versa. 'So always treat others as you would like them to treat you.' That is the golden rule as laid down by Christ in the Sermon on the Mount.

We should always try to express our gratitude in some way or other. It may be by a look, a smile, a word, a present, a letter. Thank-you letters are very important, provided they are personal, sincere and real and not merely formal and polite. Eric Abbott, formerly Dean of Westminster, was a marvellous example in this. You could not do anything for Eric, even pay him a visit or write him a letter, without receiving a thank-you letter in return – often by the next post! And just to say 'thank you' to someone who serves you in a shop lifts that relationship for a brief moment out of the realm of the impersonal into the realm of the personal.

Gratitude is an act of love and it applies therefore to all those love-relationships which I itemized in the previous chapter. Our intimate relationships, certainly. Our casual relationships. And our pastoral relationships; for we often receive as much, if not more, than we give. Perhaps even our hostile relationships, if we can manage it – although this will take very considerable grace!

We were taught to say 'thank you' when we were children. How marvellous it would be if this half-remembered, half-forgotten childhood dictum could become an adult reality, a grateful expression of heart and mind. It may seem a little thing, but it would make such a difference to human life.

*9*

## *Perseverance*

Perseverance may sound rather a dull virtue. It lacks the adventure of faith, the expectation of hope, the attraction and challenge of love, the joy of gratitude, the excitement of courage, the quiet tranquillity of peace. Yet it is the virtue we need most of all if we are going to achieve anything, as every writer, artist, musician, indeed every worker, knows only too well. No book would ever get finished, no picture be painted, no symphony composed or any work completed, without 'the grace to persevere'. Perseverance is necessary in every department of our life, from doing the ironing to saying our prayers, from playing chess to protesting against inequality and injustice.

What, then, is perseverance? It is the determination to go on in spite of all the pressures, both interior and exterior, to give up. We set ourselves to do something, to follow some course, to practise some virtue. We begin with enthusiasm and all goes well. But then, difficulties arise and obstacles appear, or disinclination, boredom and sloth set in. And the voice of temptation whispers in our ear: 'Pack it in! What's the use? You'll never get anywhere. Give it up!' Perseverance means the persistence to press on through all the difficulties and the obstacles and to overcome our disinclination, boredom and sloth, to carry on regardless and to finish what we set out to do. This is well illustrated in a prayer for perseverance based upon some words of Sir Francis Drake:

> O Lord God, when thou givest to thy servants to endeavour any great matter, grant us also to know that it is not the beginning, but the continuing of the same unto the end, until it be thoroughly finished, which yieldeth the true glory; through him who for the finishing of thy work laid down his life, our Redeemer, Jesus Christ.

Perseverance is very much a virtue of the will. It is the victory of will over feelings. Our feelings may tempt us to waver and weaken, to despair and give up, but our will refuses to be deflected.

Once when I switched on the radio, quite by chance, Dr Anthony Clare was interviewing Maya Angelou in the programme 'In the psychiatrist's chair'. Maya Angelou is a black writer in America whose books of autobiography have become best-sellers. Among the many questions Dr Clare asked her was one about religion: 'How important is religion to you?' She answered: 'It is very, very important. The sense of the presence of God in my life here and now, the presence of God in other people.' She went on: 'I am a *practising* Christian. Just as you practise to play the piano or to be a ballet-dancer or to be anything, so I am a *practising Christian*. I practise. I often blow it! But I get up again and get back to my practising.' That is perseverance.

We shall look now at some of the key moments in our life, situations, circumstances, experiences, when we have to practise this virtue of perseverance.

First of all, *in our prayer*.

You will never get anywhere in prayer without perseverance. Prayer is a very strange activity, different from all our other activities. It demands the effort to concentrate upon a Being who is inaccessible to our ordinary senses, a Being whom we cannot see or hear or touch or taste, yet whom we believe to be real and whom we believe to be, in some mysterious way, personal. But the effort to concentrate upon such a Being demands great perseverance, because our attention keeps wandering off and has to be constantly pulled back. And after a few attempts there is the temptation to give up. It is all too difficult and demanding. Only perseverance will enable us to go on, to stick at it.

Then there are our feelings of disinclination and boredom. Sometimes we feel like praying and sometimes we don't. There is the temptation to pray only when we feel like it or seem to get something out of it. But this is to make God subjective and not objective. It is believing in ourselves, our own feelings and satisfactions, not in God and in the reality of his love. This is not true prayer. True prayer is the expression of our faith and our love. But we shall only be able to follow this way if our will can conquer our feelings: in other words, if we persevere.

Again, we may go through periods of dryness and darkness in our prayer. We may experience what St John of the Cross called 'the dark night of the soul'. In this situation it is very easy to get our sums wrong;

to imagine that we have lost our faith, or conclude that perhaps there is no God after all. This would be a pity, because what God is really doing is turning off the heat and switching out the light in order to draw us into a deeper union with himself, below the level of our surface feelings, knowledge and insight. But to keep going in the dark, through the cold and the desert, demands immense perseverance. For the temptation to despair and to give up is very strong. Only perseverance will keep us going.

No wonder Baron von Hügel wrote: 'It is perseverance in the spiritual life, on and on, across the years and the changes of our moods and trials, health and environment; it is this that supremely matters.'

Then there are *our love-relationships*.

As we saw in Chapter 7, on love, we have many such love-relationships. And perseverance is necessary in each one of them.

It is necessary in our intimate relationships. Marriage will not stand the test of time, nor the interior and exterior pressures, without it. I am always suspicious of people who say 'We've been married for thirty years and we've never had a cross word yet'. Either they have very bad memories or they are both placid cabbages! It often happens that people marry someone of a different temperament and this can be positively fulfilling. But it has its negative side. Temperaments can clash. There can be crossed wires and misunderstandings, arguing at cross-purposes, living with 'unreal' people. Most marriages I know go through periods of 'stormy weather', to quote the title of a popular song of the 1930s. There is also the possibility of becoming infatuated with someone else and the temptation to be unfaithful. Only perseverance will enable us to withstand these pressures and enable our marriage to endure and to grow in depth. There is a crucifixion–resurrection pattern running through our intimate relationships, especially through marriage. Alexander Solzhenitsyn wrote in *The First Circle*:

> There is nothing predictable about relations between men and women – they have no set course and there are no laws to govern them. They sometimes reach such a dead end that there's nothing to do but sit down and howl; everything that could be said has been said, all arguments have been exhausted. But then, at a chance meeting of eyes, the blank wall may suddenly crumble away, and where all was darkness there is light and an easy path along which two people can walk again . . .

But we shall not experience the joy of resurrection if we do not persevere through the pain of crucifixion.

Perseverance is necessary in *our casual relationships*. Love involves a constant effort to remember that our neighbour whom we meet casually in the road, at the bus stop, outside the school, in the supermarket, at a committee meeting, in church, is in fact a person, equally valued and loved by God as we are. We have to remember to treat each one accordingly, resisting the temptation to ignore them or to treat them as expendable. But all this requires perseverance in our attitude towards people.

Perseverance is necessary in *our hostile relationships*. As Jesus pointed out, anyone can love those who love you. The test of love is whether you can go on loving in spite of dislike, prejudice, rebuffs, despisings, rejections, let-downs, being taken for granted. This is how James Baldwin put it in *Another Country*: 'I think you can begin to *become* admirable if, when you're hurt, you don't try to pay back . . . Perhaps if you can accept the pain that almost kills you, you can use it, you can become better . . . otherwise you just get stopped with whatever it was that ruined you and you make it happen over and over again.' But the temptation to get your own back, the temptation of revenge, however counter-productive, is very strong. To resist it, to keep the door open and not to close it, to endeavour to go on loving in spite of all the hurt and the pain, demands immense perseverance.

Perseverance is necessary in what I have called *our pastoral relationships*, our availability to be with people in trouble, to listen to them, to try to uphold and support them. This is a very wearing business. It is very demanding of our time. It is a strain upon our resources. It drains our nervous energy. And there comes the temptation, after a time, to withdraw the helping hand, to be 'out' when the doorbell or the telephone rings. To carry on being available, to continue to give of our time and energy, to keep our understanding alight and our sympathy alive, involves great perseverance in love.

Perseverance is necessary in *our social and political relationships*, our concern with the structures of society which affect the lives of people for good or ill. It is also required in what I call *our environmental relationships*, our care and responsibility for God's creation. For, as John Donne wrote: 'No man is an Island, entire of itself, every man is a piece of the Continent, a part of the Main . . . I am involved with Mankind.' And this involvement with mankind, indeed with the whole of creation, will involve us in confrontation and conflict with those powers and forces which threaten mankind and threaten creation. Confrontation and conflict is not easy, especially for people who have a fear of blame or violence. Such people will be tempted to run away. Only perseverance will keep them in line, ready to protest and fight against injustice and exploitation in spite of their fear. Again, vested interests are so powerful, so strong, that we are tempted to despair and give up the fight. What can *we* do with our pathetic bows and arrows against such battalions armed with the latest technological weapons? Give up the struggle and settle for a nice quiet life! But then we shall have ceased to be 'a part of the Main . . . involved with Mankind', responsible stewards of God's creation. Moreover, as Fr John Dalrymple has written, 'The distinctive contribution of Christians to the struggle for peace and justice has to be hope. A glance at the crucifix on the wall should always be sufficient to remind us that God is not defeated, in the long term, by the force of human selfishness, however much the short-term prospect is "hopeless". Since the resurrection we have no need to run away from Gethsemane when the cause seems lost' (*The Cross a Pasture*). But in order to stay in Gethsemane and to move on to Calvary, hope needs to be allied to perseverance. We have to persevere in hope, or we shall never experience the resurrection.

In all our love-relationships, as Dr Somerset-Ward wrote, 'perseverance is the surest sign of love'.

Then there is *our acceptance of circumstances*.

'You know the rarest thing in the world, Ninette?'

asked a psychiatrist of a young painter, in Morris West's novel, *Daughter of Silence*. He then proceeded to answer his own question. 'A man or woman wise enough to look the world in the eye and accept it, good or bad, for what it is at that moment.' This, of course, is 'abandonment to divine providence', leaving the past to the mercy of God and the future to his providence and giving oneself wholly to, accepting, 'the sacrament of the present moment'. This is what Jean-Pierre de Caussade taught people to do in eighteenth-century France. It is a very positive attitude to life, the living expression of our faith and hope. Is it all that rare, as the psychiatrist thought? I suppose that depends upon our experience of people. We tend to generalize about people from the limited number whom we know – our friends, our colleagues, our patients. There is always, of course, the choice: to accept our circumstances or to rebel against them. Acceptance means to accept who we are and what we are and where we are; to do the best we can in the circumstances there are. Rebellion, on the other hand, means to kick against circumstances or to run away from them, to be afraid to face up to things, to retreat into unreality and wishful thinking, to be for ever saying 'if only'. The if-only syndrome. If only I were different, if only I had the qualifications, if only I were married, if only I were not married, if only I lived in the country, if only I lived in the town, if only I could retire, if only I were younger. The choice between acceptance of our circumstances and rebellion against them is basically a choice between perseverance and despair. To despair is to lose all hope, to be beaten by circumstances, to give up. Perseverance is the will to go on, 'taking life in one's stride', one day at a time, one foot in front of the other, refusing to be beaten, refusing to despair. Perseverance hangs on to faith and hope in all weathers, in sunshine and in storm. It never gives up. You can see what a tough virtue perseverance is!

Then there are *our temptations*.

Our temptations are a bore because they are usually the same. We each have a vulnerability to particular temptations. These may be sensual or mental or spiritual. They may be temptations to pride and selfishness or to fear and despair. Temptation itself is not sin. It is a choice. This choice takes many forms with different people, but basically it is a choice between pleasing ourselves, doing what we want, at the expense of God and other people. Moreover, our temptations keep recurring. It is like housework – dusting, cleaning, washing-up. Where *does* that dust come from? Those plates *will* go on piling up in the kitchen sink after every meal. And we get fed up with the effort of coping with the same old thing over and over again. How do we cope with temptation? There is only one way and that is to switch our mind off the thought the moment we are aware of it and to switch it on to something else; in other words, to change the subject. But this we have to do over and over again because the thought keeps coming back, like the dust and the dirty dishes, and after a few miserable attempts comes the temptation to despair and to give up trying to resist. This is when we most need the virtue of perseverance to make us go on fighting. For it *is* a fight, 'it's a battlefield' – to quote the title of one of Graham Greene's novels. Only perseverance will enable us to be victorious.

Soldiers of Christ, arise,
And put your armour on.

Fight the good fight with all thy might.

All those hymns with their martial imagery are really a plea for perseverance. For perseverance is a virtue of the will, driving us to 'stick at it', to go on resisting.

And crown thy gifts with grace to persevere.

For only perseverance will win the day.
And finally, there are *our failures*.

Our failures are almost always a signal for depression, if not for despair. This may arise from pride: 'How are the mighty fallen!' In which case, our failures are good for us. They cut us down to size. They humiliate us. They make us join the human race again as weak, humble sinners, not as superior beings. And remember, Jesus made friends with sinners, not with the proud and the self-righteous. On the other hand, it may arise from fear: 'You see, I knew it. I told you so. I am no good. I've failed again. To hell with it, then! I might as well be killed for a sheep as for a lamb.' But if we fall for that one, we shall have allowed evil to win two victories for the price of one – not only to knock us down, but to knock us out; not only to trip us up but to pitch us into the quicksand of despair. We need to remember Maya Angelou 'practising' to be a Christian. 'I practise. I often blow it! But I get up again and get back to my practising.' Spiritual writers stress the importance of such perseverance, going on in spite of failure, never giving up in despair. Martin Thornton in *English Spirituality* wrote:

'The real difference between a saint and a sinner is that the one falls, repents, and moves hopefully on towards heaven, while the other falls and stays down.' And Dom Augustin Guillerand wrote very encouragingly: 'God will know how to draw glory even from our faults. Not to be downcast after committing a fault is one of the marks of true sanctity.'

Failure itself does not matter. It is inevitable. What matters is what you do with failure. What *do* you do with it? Do you sit down in self-pity and give up? Or do you pick yourself up again and go on? Despair or perseverance? It is like climbing a mountain. It does not matter how many times you slip, so long as you pick yourself up and go on climbing. In spite of the bruises and the cuts and the torn clothes, you will eventually get to the top and be able to enjoy the view.


The natural creation gives many examples of the power of perseverance. I am writing this chapter towards the end of March. The border in our small garden is full of crocuses, pushing their way up through the hard frosty ground. The snow came, and buried them. But it did not kill them. After a few days the sun shone and there they were in all their glory, opening their petals to the warmth and light.

Here is another illustration, this time from the world of the theatre – from Shakespeare's *Macbeth*. It may seem to you a rather strange illustration. Macbeth was not a hero. He was a tragic figure: a brave, sensitive and affectionate man, snared and destroyed by ambition. Yet towards the end of the play, he has his moment of glory. His wife has died. Burnham Wood *has* come to Dunsinane – or so he thinks. In one of his last speeches, he swings between despair and perseverance. And in this tussle, perseverance wins. He will go out fighting.

> I 'gin to be a-weary of the sun,
> And wish the estate o' the world were now undone –
> Ring the alarum bell! – Blow, wind! come, wrack!
> At least we'll die with harness on our back.

# 10

## Death

In our permissive society, four-letter words are no longer daring, shocking, unmentionable. They are part of our culture, part of the scene, 'in-words'.

But there *is* a word in our permissive, materialistic, hedonist society which is unmentionable – or, at least, embarrassing – a word which shocks, a word which should not be spoken except in a whisper. It is a five-letter word. It is the word death.

This word is 'out'. We are afraid of it, embarrassed by it. It is a shadow which calls in question all our assumptions – about pleasure, about permanence, about progress, about personality. It hovers over everything. So we try not to think about it and certainly not to talk about it – unless we really have to. 'Death' is a dirty word.

Yet death is a major fact of life, our one absolute certainty. We are born to die. 'In my beginning is my end' – as T. S. Eliot wrote at the beginning of his poem *East Coker*.

You cannot really have a satisfactory philosophy of life without considering death. The way you look at death affects the way you look at life.

The unbeliever looks at death and sees it as a full-stop, a dead-end, a point of no return, the snuffing of the candle. 'When I die, I rot,' wrote Bertrand Russell.

Now this attitude *can* lead to a great appreciation of life and relationships, to a great enjoyment of beauty and a caring about the world, a caring about justice and peace, a concern about suffering. Because this life, this world, is all we have got.

But it can also lead to a thoughtless, selfish grabbing at life. 'Eat, drink and be merry, for tomorrow we die.' 'Each man for himself and the devil take (the slowest and the weakest).'

Or it can lead to a timidity about life, to gloom and anxiety, to always looking on the dark side, perpetually haunted by the fear of death.

The believer looks at death and sees it as a comma, a throughway, a gateway into Life with a capital L – Eternal Life: Life which is freer, fuller, deeper, richer than this life on earth, a life of communion with God and with each other.

Now this attitude *can* lead to a negative, puritanical approach to life, to a despising of the joys of life, an indifference to injustice and an uncaring attitude to those who suffer. This, unfortunately, is one of the blots on the pages of church history for which we should be deeply ashamed.

But it can also lead both to a deep appreciation of the beauty of God's creation and to a care and concern for other people, especially for those who suffer – after the example of the risen Christ whom we worship. Jesus obviously appreciated natural beauty: 'Behold the flowers of the field, the birds of the air.' He was also the friend of society's outcasts and sinners, and in his parable of the sheep and the goats he said: 'Inasmuch as you fed the hungry, clothed the naked, welcomed the stranger, visited the sick and those in prison, you did it [or you did not do it] to me.'

This attitude can also act as a useful yardstick by which we measure what is important and what is unimportant. I remember going – many years ago – to see a film starring Lionel Barrymore. The film was called, significantly, *You can't take it with you.*

The true believer, while enjoying life and contributing to life and measuring the true value of life here and now, also lives – and dies – with an expectation of the glory which is to come.

At the end of his great novel, *The Brothers Karamazov*, Dostoevsky wrote:

'Karamazov,' cried Kolya, 'is it really true that, as our religion tells us, we shall all rise from the dead and come to life and see one another again?' 'Certainly we shall rise again, certainly we shall see one another, and shall tell one another gladly and joyfully all that has been,' Aloysha replied, half laughing, half rapturously. 'Oh, how wonderful it will be!' Kolya cried.

That is how William Blake died – rapturously. He had been ill for about a year. Towards the end, he drew a portrait of his wife Kate. He then put it down and began to sing alleluias and songs of joy and triumph, which Mrs Blake described as being 'truly sublime in music and in verse'. Then, 'his spirit departed like the sighing of a gentle breeze'.

That is how T. S. Eliot ended his poem *East Coker*:

> We must be still and still moving
> Into another intensity
> For a further union, a deeper communion . . .
> In my end is my beginning.

Now is this belief in eternal life mere wishful thinking, a pathetic attempt to make sense of life, to redeem it from futility? Or are there reasons for believing?

It is, of course, a sheer act of faith – faith described by Kierkegaard as a leap and by Pascal as a wager. Faith is not knowledge. It is not certainty. It is a jump, a gamble. It always has to live with doubt and questioning. But only a fool would jump in the dark from a precipice, or gamble on an absolutely outside chance. You cannot prove the existence of eternal life, any more than you can prove the existence of God. Neither can you disprove it. You cannot demonstrate it scientifically. And yet I think there are reasons which help to justify making this act of faith.

### A common-sense reason

Life simply does not make sense except against a background of eternity. If there is a purpose in life at all, that purpose must surely stretch beyond death. For death calls life in question and renders it absurd.

> A tale told by an idiot
> Full of sound and fury, signifying nothing.

What a senseless waste life is, if the whole complicated process of conception, birth, growing up, education, experience, relationships, work, creativity, could be suddenly and totally obliterated by some chance accident – a stray virus, a skidding bus, a sudden heart attack, cancer.

How unjust life is for many people. There are those who are limited by physical and mental disease, frustrated by imprisoning circumstances. How unjust and unfair if that is their ultimate lot.

Very few people die absolutely happy, satisfied, fulfilled. Most people die regretfully, with ambitions which were never fulfilled, dreams which never came true, hopes which never materialized. Now unless these ambitions, dreams, hopes, longings, aches and desires are a complete fraud, an illusion, must there not be a future, a life beyond death, where they can be fulfilled and realized?

*An instinctive reason*
Rebellion against death and hope of immortality is a fairly universal instinct. Primitive man was buried with his belongings in the grave – a crude expression of belief that he was on a journey and that he would need them when he reached his journey's end. Greek philosophers regarded the immortality of the soul as one of the great basic truths. So did Immanuel Kant. The Jewish psalms are full of lament about death and later apocalyptic writers look forward to a general resurrection. St Paul described death as 'the last enemy'. Kierkegaard described it as 'a comedian'.

In our experience, every instinct has an outlet. If this is true of hunger or sex or beauty, why should it not be true of the instinct for immortality?

## A theological reason

If God is Love – and this is the heart of the Christian Gospel, the Good News that God *is* Love, a love revealed and demonstrated in the life and death of Jesus Christ – then he could not bear to lose, to be parted from, those whom he loves. For that is the nature of love. Why are we so shattered, devastated, when our husband, our wife, our son, our daughter, our intimate friends, die? Is it not because of our love, our union with them? They have become part of our-selves. Death which separates us, tears us apart, is unbearable. If this experience is true of our human, fallible loves, how much more must it be true of God who is pure, unlimited, unbreakable Love. If God was once the God of Abraham, Isaac and Jacob, must he not be their God now? If they were once precious to him, are they not precious now? For God is eternal and unchangeable, as he was in the beginning, is now and ever shall be. He is the God of the living, not of the dead. So they are alive in him.

## A Christian reason

Jesus died. Jesus was raised from the dead. The early Christians experienced a sense of union with him. In St Paul's words, 'I live, yet not I, but Christ liveth in me'. This experience has persisted all down the centuries. Without the experience of the resurrection and belief in the resurrection, there would have been no Christianity. It is recorded in St John's Gospel that Jesus said 'I go to prepare a place for you . . . that where I am you may be also'. And the next day, Good Friday, as he hung dying on the cross, he said to the thief (or criminal – or perhaps he was what we call a terrorist) hanging next to him, 'Today, you shall be with me in paradise'. Because of his belief in the resurrection of Christ, John Donne could write in his *Divine Poems*:

> Death be not proud, though some have called thee
> Mighty and dreadful, for, thou art not soe

> One short sleepe past, wee wake eternally,
> And death shall be no more; death, thou shalt die.

'In my end is my beginning.'

All right, then. If there is life after death, what will it be like? I think we can say two things by faith.

First, it will be a fully personal life, a life of real communion with God and with each other. We can say this because we believe that God created persons – body and soul – and because 'the Word' (spiritual) 'was made flesh'. Christians believe not merely in immortality, the indestructible spirit of a person escaping from the prison of the body and being absorbed into the Universal Spirit, like a drop of water in the ocean. Christians believe in resurrection, the raising-up of a real, individual person with a body to be a person with – a means of recognition and communication. That is what a body is and this is what we mean when we say in the Creed, 'I believe in the resurrection of the body'.

Secondly, it will be life of a particular depth and quality. Not 'everlasting life', which is a boring, quantitative term, but 'eternal life', which is qualitative.

There are moments in this life of particular depth

and quality, moments when the clock stops and we are lifted out of ourselves and experience something 'out of this world'. It may be a moment of great beauty, or a moment of great love. Perhaps these fleeting moments of intense experience are hints, foretastes of what eternal life will be like.


About the geography, the climate, the furniture, the fashion of life after death, we are agnostics. We do not know. And we do not need to know. All we need is to trust God.

An old man lay dying in Scotland. He asked his doctor what he thought it would be like 'on the other side'. The doctor did not quite know what to say. Then he was suddenly given a cue. There was a sound of barking and scratching at the bedroom door. The doctor said, 'Do you hear that? It's my dog. I left him downstairs, but he's getting restless. He wants to come in. Now, he doesn't know what he will find in this room. He hasn't been here before. All he knows is that I am here and he trusts me.'

# Suggested Reading

(This is simply a list of books which have helped me personally and which seem to touch on the matter of this book.)

Angelou, Maya, *I Know Why the Caged Bird Sings*. Virago 1984.
— *Gather Together in My Name*. Virago 1985.
— *Singing and Swingin' and Gettin' Merry like Christmas*. Virago 1985.
— *The Heart of a Woman*. Virago 1986.
— *All God's Children Need Travelling Shoes*. Virago 1987.
Baillie, John, *And the Life Everlasting*. Wyvern Books 1961.
Bonhoeffer, Dietrich, *Letters and Papers from Prison*. Fontana 1959.
Dominian, Jack, *Depression*. DLT and Fontana 1976.
Eliot, T. S., *Four Quartets*. Faber 1959.
Elliott, Charles, *Praying the Kingdom: Towards a Political Spirituality*. DLT 1985.
ffrench-Beytagh, Gonville, *A Glimpse of Glory*. DLT 1986.
Hughes, G. W., *God of Surprises*. DLT 1985.

Leech, Kenneth, *Spirituality and Pastoral Care*. Sheldon Press 1986.

Lewis, C. S., *A Grief Observed*. Faber 1966.

Llewelyn, Robert (ed.), *Julian, Woman of Our Day*. DLT 1985.

Merton, Thomas, *Conjectures of a Guilty Bystander*. Sheldon Press 1977.

Mitchell, Laura, *Simple Relaxation*. John Murray 1977. (This book on methods for easing tension is now being revised, by the author, and should be published towards the end of 1987.)

Nouwen, Henri, *In the House of the Lord*. DLT 1986.

Thompson, Jim, *Half Way*. Fount Paperbacks 1986.

Toynbee, Philip, *Part of a Journey*. Collins 1982.

Vanstone, W. H., *Love's Endeavour, Love's Expense*. DLT 1977.

Williams, H. A., *Tensions*. Mitchell Beazley 1976.

— *The Joy of God*. Mitchell Beazley 1979.